The Journey Continues

Sequel to *Journey of a Lifetime*

Also by
Merle Stubbs

Journey of a Lifetime: A Group Story

An account of the journey of a group
through more than thirty years work.

**We stand with the Christ in the Fire of Love
To the Glory of the One**

The Journey Continues

Sequel to Journey of a Lifetime

Merle Stubbs

SYDNEY GOODWILL
UNIT OF SERVICE LIMITED
AUSTRALIA

Sydney Goodwill Unit of Service Ltd.

PO Box 627, Caringbah, NSW 1495 Australia
Phone   61 2 9540 2391
Fax   61 2 9524 0025
E-mail goodwill@sydneygoodwill.org.au
Website www.sydneygoodwill.org.au

First published 2002

© Merle Stubbs 2002

Except as provided by the Copyright Act 1968, no part of this publication may be reproduced by any process, stored in a retrieval system or transmitted in any form or by any means without the prior permission of the author. Requests and enquiries should be directed to Sydney Goodwill Unit of Service Ltd.

The National Library of Australia Cataloguing-in-Publication

Stubbs, Merle, 1931-.
The Journey Continues.

ISBN 0 958 0031 0 6.

1. Occultism. 2. Spiritual life. 3. Spiritual formation.
4. Small groups - Philosophy. 5. Esoteric astrology.
I. Maver, Dorothy J. II. Sydney Goodwill Unit of Service.
III. Title.

Cat.no. 133

Editor: Dorothy J. Maver
Cover design, typesetting: G.J. Nagle

Cover image of Cygnus Loop courtesy of NASA, the European Space Agency Information Centre, and Dr. William Blair (Johns Hopkins University).

Printed by Southwood Press, New South Wales, Australia

This Book is Dedicated to the Next Race

Contents

Preface		13
Editor's Note		15
Prologue	The Vision of Oneness	16
CHAPTER ONE	What is Life?	19
CHAPTER TWO	The Group as a Single Entity	25
CHAPTER THREE	Aspects of Miniature Hierarchy	29
CHAPTER FOUR	Through: Entering the Fifth Phase	35
CHAPTER FIVE	Things Were Beginning to Happen	43
CHAPTER SIX	Across the World	57
CHAPTER SEVEN	Oneness to Synthesis	63
CHAPTER EIGHT	Movement in Identical At-one-ness	71
CHAPTER NINE	Understanding Patterns	77
CHAPTER TEN	Sensitivity	87
CHAPTER ELEVEN	Once upon a Time	93
CHAPTER TWELVE	Anecdotes along the Road	107
CHAPTER THIRTEEN	The Learning Process	119
CHAPTER FOURTEEN	Unfolding Realisation The Fifth Phase of the Group	129
Epilogue	The Future World	135

Learning to fly

One memorable day when I was ten years old the school Headmistress was looking after the class for an absent teacher. The class was mapping the Australian continent on graph paper. Providing one stayed within the guidelines one was assured of making the outline continuous and of correct shape. However, this one ten year old arrived at the west coast from the east and Australia no longer looked quite the same. So she walked out to the front desk and said to the Headmistress, "Mrs Rose, I can't make this fit." Mrs Rose replied, "There is no such thing as can't!" And the small girl immediately thought, "I can't fly" but did not dare voice that opinion. Mrs Rose knew everything! We must take her statement seriously. And so one small girl discovered that we could indeed fly as the true beings we are and within our natural dimension. The physical world is then no prison, but the realm in which we learn, grow and serve the Race.

Come fly with me…

PREFACE

A short time following the publication of *Journey of a Lifetime: A Group Story* it became evident in our awareness that this first book was introductory, serving as a platform from which to present the deeper significances of the work and of the understanding now available within the group life and work into the future. A second 'statement', emerging as a second book, began to appear deep in thought levels, insinuating itself into and through the expression of the group consciousness and its point of focused activity.

The newly emerging thought gained in clarity as we noted its movement onward from previously defined states of awareness, group issues and requirements, as shared with readers in *Journey of a Lifetime*. The attempts to define group issues in word forms had endowed us with a yardstick, a tool of comparison, by which we could more readily identify the change, the movement and deepening in the group consciousness, and the demands now made upon the Group in terms of ongoing and future service.

For example: A key understanding that governed the way of working from the Group's inception more than 30 years ago was termed 'working from the inside out'. Rather than holding focus upon the outer planes of living and endeavouring to penetrate the inner levels, the Group transferred its consciousness and its living processes to the inner levels and observed and directed life and operations from that 'elevated' viewpoint, thus affording untrammelled vision of human expression and affairs, of group work and personnel, and of the new possibilities emerging into expression in a New Day upon our planet.

By comparison, this new moment so recently emerging in the group awareness in the middle of the year 2001 saw the Group move through into much deeper areas of understanding. The attempt to find wording to define the experience of seemingly formless states,

* The capitalised letter G throughout this book identifies the Group whose story is told in these pages.

and the ensuing demands and significances in the group work, was even more challenging than before. We had now entered an area, an awareness, in which our group life, incorporating each and every individual member, was one with Life itself. This is no mystical state. It is a state of awareness which is clearly known and in which we are conscious participants. It is so much deeper in realisation than 'working from the inside out' although that experience may be a useful or even necessary preliminary. It is an obvious 'next step' as the Life aspect begins to supersede emphasis upon the consciousness aspect in human possibilities.

We noted also that the first statement of the Group, *Journey of a Lifetime*, briefly outlined the Group's journey from its early days, through time, from *the past* up to the present moment of writing. But now we stand at that point where we recognise we are expressing, working, in and into *the future*. We contact new energies. We anticipate new expressions of Life in descent into our planet, outpicturing in new, more adequate and suitable forms for the future ongoing life in Aquarius. For the creation of such forms we all are responsible. The new life cannot be pressured into outmoded forms.

In this book we will endeavour to share our experience with all who may wish to travel this continuing journey with us and with the myriad other servers upon this Way. We will endeavour to address this movement in awareness through the various aspects we are identifying, and even this is merely a beginning.

And so, the Group moves onward in Life from the first four phases identified in *Journey of a Lifetime* and enters into *Phase Five*.

* * * * *

Editor's Note

When Merle suggested there was a second book I posed the question, "Is there really another book?" She assured me "It is sitting over my head," and forthwith wrote the preface in answer. I then asked, "Why write this book?" and she replied, "It is demanding expression. The world group stands with such equilibrium and knowing, that the future is assured. Because the book is there. It tells me that this is what needs to be said as we move into this 21st century. Humanity is ready to take yet another step.

"We know, and it has been written decades ago, that the Life aspect is to supersede the Son or consciousness aspect. When are we going to address this? This is emerging in the group consciousness as experience, as a very clear recognition, and just as we wrote the first book to share with those who may wish to and could profit at all by it, we also presented the same statement that the Life aspect is that which we must next embrace and express. But we've moved further into this and because this is beginning to express through the Group we find a new requirement. It is written in an attempt to define it in words – to put into another book to share the next step with those who may understand.

"The first book just touched on these possibilities and saw the Group readying through its first four phases to take this next step. And we never know until we get somewhere what it looks like. Now this Group is fully integrated into one entity as a result of its first four phases, and enters its fifth phase of expression. As a single entity merged with Life itself, it begins to understand and to express what is needed in this next moment. Thus a second book is called forth. There's an internal pressure that demands that it appear out here in word form."

And so the journey continues.

PROLOGUE

The Vision of Oneness

Why is oneness so important to consider? It is the basic reality of the system. Let us take a trip into the formless worlds, into those states that *are* before we find anything made manifest. What if we were a Logos creating a world designed to bring its inhabitants through many and various stages to a realisation of their relationship, their identification with that Logos, their Father? And then on to the knowledge of the purpose behind it all?

The Logos in deep thought and meditation plans his creation, his design, and breathes it forth on the wings of sound into actual being. In its descent from the rarity of its subtle origin it begins to take on substance through the planes, increasingly growing in density and diversity ever outward and downward, taking on colour, depth, matter, form, and all imbued with the divine essence of life.

Long are the ages his children wander through this world unknowing but gradually developing senses of apprehension and recognising with a growing intelligence the nature of their environment and their relationship within it. But they have long since forgotten their divine origin in their necessity to become identified within the created world which offers them the opportunity themselves to become conscious creators just as their Father.

~ ~ ~

So the Logos, after many aeons, decided to send Enlightened Ones to teach his children and bring them more rapidly to the realisation of their true estate. The Enlightened Ones arrived among the children at various intervals and taught them what they next needed to understand to take further steps along the Way. But it always seemed to happen that, because of the stages of development of the children at any time, when the Teacher left, the children were inclined to embroider and distort the Teaching applying it in the denser world rather than within the realms of their growth in consciousness. So the Teaching invariably became materialised whereas if the true meaning had been apprehended and the children had truly absorbed its essence *into their consciousness* then they would have expressed its truth outward into and through their lives, more closely and truly representing the message the Teacher had brought. The world of the form-life had taken such a strong hold!

Because of this failure to understand the nature of consciousness and that they were actually spiritual beings, a further complication arose. The various Teachers who visited the world encapsulated the living essence of the Teaching in a variety of forms and representations. The children, ever clinging to the form, focused on the differences they observed between the forms of the Teaching and failed to see the same living plan of their Father running through every form. And so an enmity sprang up between them and they pitted one Teacher, one form of the Teaching, against another. They even took up arms against one another, brother and sister fighting over forms, oblivious of their common heritage and the spiritual life they all shared.

But there were always those in any time who understood the truth, who saw it shining through the forms. They held it in their hearts and often banded together in groups and protected the true essence. Thus the Wisdom remained in the world, the great open secret, hidden from those who saw only with the material eyes, but ever present and giving life to all.

Eventually there came a time when the forces of truth and of error, of reality and of distortion, were of equal balance and the race stood at a place where they faced a decision of which path to take. One led in the direction of the spiritual kingdoms and their true home and the other into even deeper materialism and conflict. The first embraced the reality of the oneness of all life, of all peoples, and the other knew nothing but separation. It was a time of great crisis and choice stood clearly open as never before.

However, the many who understood the spiritual path, aided by the Teachers standing with them in the subtle dimension, were now in such strength as to enable the light to break through into the world, illumining consciousness and revealing the reality of Oneness within which all existed. At the same time, the shadows of separation became obvious but those who dwelt within them clung to them and turned away from the light. But the world of shadows was no longer supportable by those who could see and who proceeded to work with vigour and with insight to restore the plan of their Father and to prepare the way for the Teacher who was to come in their time.

Chapter One
What is Life?

What is Life? What is it that appears to have gone when something dies? Where is it? What is it that is obviously present at birth and in growth? We say 'it just is' but cannot truly begin to define it. We can see how it differs from the second aspect of Deity, Love, or from any qualities we care to name. It is not qualified by anything. It is not limited by anything. It cannot be owned exclusively by anything or anyone.

The recognition of Life moves us on from the teaching of 'sharing' only as an expression of Love. Once we enter a conscious awareness of the nature of Life itself we have realised that 'sharing' is an inevitable and normal expression of all life. It cannot be otherwise. As we stand within the Life aspect our expression through all planes of being functions for the good of the whole and the individual expresses his or her potential through individual capacities, in cooperation with their group and directed with love and wisdom.

In such a scenario we can offset the prevalence of the past, in its emphasis on the individual capacity for creating grand personal egos, and educating and training everyone to a narrow system which failed to bring forth into accepted expression the valuable potential of those who differed from the strictly or perceived required expression. Of course, recognising separation, this system has trained people to take their positions in the marketplace of competition found on the planet at this time throughout the many and varied avenues of human involvement and endeavour. It is now time for the recognition of that cooperative interaction born of our realisation of the Oneness of life.

One cannot take life. It is neither created nor destroyed. We express in life and through life, but do we express Life? So what is it we are talking about? Who can put words to it? We may think of life in terms of that energy that enlivens everything. Nothing has existence without life. So do we express it or just through it? If we say life has a purpose then in a sense we have made it into an entity. Is it an entity? Is it energy? Is it both?

Life just is. And entities great and small express Life according to their level of awareness. There is a vast difference between a member of humanity expressing Life and the Logos of the planet expressing Life and yet it is the same Life. Life is and for aye remains.

What does it mean to work within the Life aspect?

A group does nothing unless it can reveal something through its life expression. This is not premeditated or organised but is an automatic and inevitable outflow of the vitality of its very Being. This realisation transcends those older and better understood group methods wherein people gather around an organised working group, or students gather around a teacher, with an emphasis upon personal relationship and upon the receiving of instruction. That there is personal emphasis in such groups may be denied but how often the personalities of those concerned may be to the fore in one way or another.

We all as workers in this New Day recognise that unless we truly apprehend the new elements emerging in this time as Life speaks anew, unless this vision inspires us to embrace new approaches to truth, we are in danger of endeavouring to press that which is newly emerging into outmoded forms. Unsupported and uninformed by the new life energies, these forms will disappear.

What is it that is hovering over the consciousness of the workers of the world who in turn are responsible for identifying and presenting that which will reveal the next step for humanity as a whole?

We are moving beyond the demand for personal readiness or even for group unity or harmony of relationships. These qualities necessarily exist within the group life.

What is it that these workers need to understand? Where to focus their being. In what though? What is it? That is the question. In the first book *Journey of a Lifetime* we asked the question 'What is it that we see seeking emergence?' The approach we now take is to identify a way of being, *where* we need to be focused. It is difficult to clearly elucidate using words like 'where' unless we understand that we are using 'where' to indicate position 'in a state of being' – in a state of awareness. We understand that not only are we not in any way separate from this state of being, from what Life is expressing at this moment, but that we are also *fully conscious* of it. There is completeness about this. We cannot just have little snippets of information from around the edges. This is a state of being before diversification.

We need to stand within this being. This is taking a deeper plunge. This is working from very Being itself. This is working from and within the Life aspect, not just 'from the inside out' as was understood earlier in the group life and expression. The group entity itself is capable of this movement. Group members may understand in varying degrees but everyone is incorporated within the group entity which moves onward *as a group*. As never before the importance of the group is realised.

What is being revealed at this moment is that capacity to identify, and consciously, within a state of being. And what that says in essence, and what that says in expression, is that we are *conscious* participants within it – within the emerging expression of Life in our time. Life needs its expressive agents all the way out into planetary expression, flowing outward through the many world groups.

In *Journey of a Lifetime* we realised when we asked 'What is emerging and how does it emerge?' that we were not separate from it; we were involved within it. Now we realise that *we must become its living expression*. This is another step, a new phase, in the group life. There is much more we do not yet apprehend. There are still unknown factors. It is said that not even the highest initiate sees with any clarity the next thing that lies ahead of him or her. There is a vital awareness that we stand in readiness as a group at the point of revelation on the edge of Aquarius, group with group with group, within the one great world group of workers.

Life-sharing

When we consider working within the Life aspect we are not talking about the personal life or the soul life but of that which is beyond them both, the all-inclusive Self. We are faced with the necessity to comprehend the nature of 'identification' as we enter the realm of synthesis. It is said that we cannot begin to understand what identification is unless or until we have experienced identical at-one-ness with even one other person; once experienced we find a door opening. When we enter into anything that exactly expresses a principle, even though it may not be the totality of its possibility, we have heard the 'sound' that enables us progressively to enter the fullness of it – of identification with it. We come to a point where we realise 'there are *no other* selves'.

From the realisation that we are identically at-one we share life. It is life expressing and we have no other concern or wish than to express that; it is beyond any personal or lesser desire. Then opens increasingly deeper, expanded realisation of what identification means. When we start off with the realisation of identical at-one-ness with one person we cannot help but proceed because there is nothing separate or separative within this awareness. We come to the place of knowing 'there are no other selves' and it matters not whether other people we meet think there are other selves. We know there are not.

As life-sharing proceeds, expands, deepens, we are aware of the vastness of that centre within which we dwell. Because we are experiencing identical at-one-ness we find that every other being is part of it. Where is there ever a division? Divisions are only created by limited awareness. And, my friends, there is no division. There is diversity. That is not division. That is expression.

We are all expressions of the one Life at varying stages of realisation or 'unrealisation'. It is the most freeing experience one can ever possibly imagine – whenever we enter into anything we break through into a new area of consciousness. We break through into a far vaster dimension than our first touch with it. Having grasped a principle, understanding how it operates, we can employ it, set it in motion. But the old problem exists: *to break through into something new we must leave something else behind.* And this is where people are reluctant. "I might lose my identity." "I may lose my comfort zone, my security blanket – the things that hedge me around." " I don't have to face the big, wide universe. The big, wide world was bad enough."

We stand at a challenging and opportune stage, because of the direct impact of Shamballa energy made upon human consciousness in the year 2000 and because of the recognition that identification, the monadic, the will aspect, the first aspect of Deity, is making its presence felt. It is seen emerging through group statement and if you are a worker then it is a matter of conscious choice. We elect to move with it and break through or stay where we are which has never been so uncomfortable as it now is. If people but understood, it is far more uncomfortable to stay back than it is to break through. These are always the illusions.

When we break through we break through into such a greater sense of freedom we wonder why we ever held back. It does, however, bring its own responsibilities. It does not allow anyone to be indifferent, lazy or inactive. What is indifference, laziness or inaction any more? We are living. This is life. Life and motion are synonymous terms. How can we be static anywhere? How can we arrest our movement forward? It is unthinkable. How can we choose to stay in a confined space when Life beckons? This is where it is.

And so it was with such thoughts and deepening understanding that the Group entered a *fifth phase* in its life experience and in its work. And every member knew that all were a part of a single group entity.

CHAPTER TWO
The Group as a Single Entity

It began to dawn upon the Group that the group Entity itself had moved on. It no longer had concern for or was even aware of the individuals that comprise the Group. Just as the soul does not care or notice whether the personality is happy or sad, so the group Entity expressing at outer levels and comprised of all the individuals concerned, does not give two hoots whether the individual within the group form is happy, sad, fulfilled, noticed or whatever. The group members truly began to understand what is meant when it is said that the whole is more important than the part. It was recognised as a necessity and as inevitable. The individual members, merged with the Group, became expressions of the group purpose, life and work, the parts incorporated within the whole.

Just as we notice that whenever we act upon recognised opportunity and move into action guided by spiritual impression or new thought, doors seem to open before us – new and broader vistas appear – ofttimes revealed through various events or happenings, so the Group found life making revelation in various ways.

In the usual course of events we may not have seen significance in certain happenings but with the Group in rhythm with a new phase and acting as one, a single being, subtle pointers were apprehended in their import by all members simultaneously.

When *Journey of a Lifetime* was published a new realisation, a new phase, was already beginning to emerge in the Group awareness. At a meditation meeting held in March 2001 the group member who had prepared the talk for the evening found she had forgotten to bring the talk with her. It was a most unusual meeting. 'The talk' was given by almost everyone present rather than one person speaking to and for the rest. Although it was not considered that we need continue this method in the future, it did not go unnoticed by anyone that the Group symbolically and actually had become a single entity. And one group member did comment on the distinction between 'preparation' and 'readiness' as each one spoke from the inner reservoir.

As this realisation continued to unfold everyone became aware of the fact that the group is an entity complete in itself. As an entity it has its own life. And all realised that we are *all* moving together within this entity. It does not matter where anyone's point of realisation may be. There is a sense of responsibility that this is a task we are all performing together.

The Not-self

Moving another step onward in the work can always bring its challenges and difficulties. A challenge that confronts some individuals in the work is presented by the reaction of personalities, closely associated with them in their outer lives, who sense the movement and fear they are being left behind or not included in common interests. These workers become aware of clinging hands.

We cannot respond to emotional coercion but it is another thing to observe these close associates upon the inner plane and ask 'Do they know themselves as they truly are?' If we can 'hold them' within that inner area where they really do know themselves and then turn our eyes to the clinging hands, we will see that these hands exist in the dimension of the not-self and we may recognise what a disservice we actually do if our response is in the emotional world. We help no one to move onward by reinforcing their misunderstanding of the true nature of life.

This understanding is also applicable to the group life itself. At the point the Group in question now stands we note that the group Entity does not address or acknowledge the not-self. If the group vehicles are the sum total of the vehicles of the individuals in the group then the group entity initially had a not-self. The group entity is going through expansions of consciousness, through into greater awareness, a continuing expansion, and treats its vehicles in much the same way as an individual at this point. That is why the group entity no longer acknowledges the not-self.

The group entity is no longer interested in individual affairs or what any individual may still be addressing in the lesser life. This does not mean that there may not be someone in the group doing battle with something in the outer life. However, where the group entity may have made allowance before, now it no longer sees such battles or knows them to exist. At this point the individuals in the group are unified in service within the group entity and there is no interest in or focus upon separate individual considerations.

This is a great advance as far as the value of that group is concerned and therefore what it can do and achieve in the work. It has arrived at a point where it is a most usable group and it is the responsibility of every individual member to refuse admittance of 'noise' into the group life. And what is 'noise' but the intrusion of personal thoughts and requirements? This is not a demand for perfection.

If, for comparison, we consider that great group, the spiritual Hierarchy, we will note that all are incorporated – from the Christ at the centre to the most inexperienced workers at the periphery. Thus all areas and levels of consciousness are represented and available in the work – from the highest realisation to the understanding closer to and needed by humanity as a whole. This great serving group therefore has within it every valuable quality, needed knowledge, and experience to further the divine Plan for the time. Personal affairs, however, are never admitted into the Ashram.

CHAPTER THREE
Aspects of Miniature Hierarchy

It may be said that Hierarchy is a structure, a way of working. Hierarchy, being the heart centre of the planet, has the Christ as its great leader at the heart of Hierarchy itself. This is the method whereby the work proceeds out from the very central point which carries the purpose, the plan, the work for this period of time, outward into expression through the ranks of the initiates and disciples, all the way out until it becomes available to humanity to take human affairs and understanding into the next and higher phase of expression.

Any group working in line with Hierarchy is working in the same way: From the point of inspiration, moving out through coordination of that contacted and into a point of application in the world work. So the structure might be seen symbolically from the point of focus (or heart) at the centre with a series of concentric circles all the way out to the periphery, enabling movement outward. At the same time, the centre remains protected from those areas further out which do not share the same degree of realisation, and yet all have the same opportunity to work with the *same energies* out into expression.

In the first phase of the Group, over thirty years ago, we understood the expression of a miniature Hierarchy in its most obvious interpretation. This may apply to any group. Here we have a group of people drawn together in service and attentive to impression from the subjective planes and their inner group. Here you have people recognising where everyone stands; we have people with various capacities and degrees of understanding and the group as a unity functions under the inspiration provided by those who may, coordinated within the field of the work by others and thence carried on outward into the point of application in the world of human affairs and expression. *There* is a miniature Hierarchy in operation.

When we moved into the second phase of the Group, into the public arena, it was a very different environment requiring more formal structures although the subjective work continued unabated behind the scenes. Miniature Hierarchy took on yet another significance, a further aspect, in terms of the group work. It could be seen that there was an emphasis upon its protective nature and capacity, protection of the central focus of the newly established work, the seed that must not be disturbed or allowed to die under any circumstances. No personality disruption or interference could be allowed to hinder or destroy. Again the protection is understood in terms of 'concentric circles' – everyone is included and incorporated but nothing is allowed to disturb that centre.

A third aspect of miniature Hierarchy started to appear within the group awareness as the Group began to recognise the Life aspect and move into an understanding of life-sharing. It was realised that the whole group moves together, and as a group. It makes no difference that the group members may be at various points of understanding or realisation. We are not considering differences or separate states. The group at this point is an entity in its own right.

Humanity itself is a group, the world disciple, progressing through time and growing in conscious awareness through life experience on this planet and this is not clearly seen while we focus our sight myopically on specific individuals, groups or peoples at any particular time. Humanity also moves 'together and as a group'.

We may observe the same story with the spiritual Hierarchy of the planet. We narrow down the true picture if we believe that the Hierarchy's only concern is to assist a struggling humanity. The Hierarchy has a goal of its own and onward they move, together and as a group, incorporating in their conscious awareness not only the planes upon which humanity lives and expresses but also those planes higher and beyond the average human awareness. They incorporate the five planes of human evolution within their conscious expression. It matters not at what stage its members all may express. It is a unified group and we need not study the 'cells' within it.

At this point in a group's life previous emphasis upon individuals must have dropped below the levels of conscious focus in the recognition or overwhelming realisation that the group is an entity, and the whole group can and must go onward together as a unit. Is it any surprise that the group Entity itself at this stage has so lost interest in any individual within the group that it never occurs in consciousness to think in such a way? That certain individuals may at times be uncomfortable may be true but if that is so then they are uncomfortable and the Group is moving on along its life path regardless. There are those in the group who are so decentralised and so captured by the vision that is the group's work that the movement onward of the whole group is assured.

Basically, those workers who are drawn together in group service have karmic links of group relationship from the past and although at times some may appear to drop out of the work they are never really lost to the group, they cannot opt out, and will return in another moment in time or another incarnation to take up the task together with their group. And those who may step through the illusory veil of death are still part of the group. *This* is a group. We are a group because we have known one another through time, because we have karmic working links. This constitutes the realisation that the whole group not only can go together but that they do. And the group Entity comes to a practical, demonstrating realisation of that understanding.

The group in Aquarius, just like Hierarchy, moves as a group. Any group that has come to a point where it can operate as a miniature Hierarchy knows that everyone is not at the same stage of awareness but that they are all so integrated into that one life that they move together and as a group. Then they understand that they will one day arrive together at that ultimate realisation where the planes we now exist on drop below the level of consciousness and another great vista, a new adventure in Life experience, will open before the group.

Another understanding which dawns upon the Group at the present stage is that the teachings and principles that guided the Group through its earlier stages, now absorbed in their essence within the group awareness, drop into the background of the group life. They are known as guiding principles and working tools but it is recognised that there is no longer any necessity for the Group to discuss these matters which allows for 'free space' through which the newly emerging realisations or revelation may enter. Discussion within the Group enters into that which *can be* known and not merely that which *is* known.

Since the emphasis is not on the individual in the Group, as each one may speak or contribute, the speaking is not of oneself but represents the group expression. When truly understood, as group members speak they are not relaying something of themselves but that which is newly emerging within the next stage of expression.

Perhaps the best symbolic illustration we may find to describe such a unified group, a miniature Hierarchy, is the human hand. The hand has to have everything operating otherwise there is some impediment to free movement and dexterity, therefore to what can be achieved. One cannot perform any task properly with the hand if each part is not working together with the others as a cooperative whole. But those fingers do not have to think about how they will work in cooperation. They just do. They are a group entity. They may operate singly with certain movements but the fingers and thumb respond automatically and in unison as they receive a message from the brain to perform any function.

Sometimes one person in the group may come to the fore for some reason or function but that is still not seen as an individual contribution; it is still a group expression of a totality. And no 'digit' considers itself better or lesser than any other because they all know that every one of them is needed, together in full functioning capacity, to perform their group task with understanding and with no loss of time or energy.

A fourth aspect of miniature Hierarchy that we may identify is that Hierarchy itself is not occupied with the present; it builds for the future. So any group expressing as a miniature Hierarchy, and as an outpost of the inner group, reflecting Hierarchical method, finds itself working for the future. Although such a group may be seen in its outer function in the work as a whole, it is truly a subjectively focused group. That which it has to convey is 'lived into being', lived into human consciousness, bearing significance for the future expression of the race. It works in and for the future – a deeper, wider, more expansive area of working than experienced before.

So here we have a group working in the world, related to the inner Ashram, working on all these planes simultaneously. This may not be seen or understood by those whose work and conscious focus lies mainly in the outer world but this does not deter the group any more than Hierarchy can be deterred. All workers are needed and fulfil their respective work within the whole. Hierarchy builds for the future and so likewise does the group that is an externalised point of the inner Ashram. All that is done is with the intent to open the way through into a wider and more expansive world.

Chapter four
Through

Entering the Fifth Phase

In the *fifth phase* of the Group's expressive life it worked at drawing through thoughts and ideas within the group operation. From the moment it was realised that the Group itself was a single Entity and as such was disinterested, unaware of, separate individuals within the Group, then almost automatically we found ourselves functioning within one consciousness, together apprehending something pressing upon our awareness, descending upon us.

The Group seemed subjectively to be held at a point of tension which was carried through and held with full conscious intent as we met together on the outer plane. And whereas at earlier phases in the Group's life we found it necessary to balance forces it was now no longer a requirement. Also the subtle senses could not now be thought of in isolation but the group Entity functioned with *the* subtle sense as one single, whole faculty.

The Group had considered the nature of Synthesis, the understanding that everything exists as one, abstract and concrete, the centre and the periphery. We had worked with the understanding of Attraction which draws and holds together all related systems including the group and groups. And we were considering the nature of Economy or that which guarantees there is no wastage of energy in onward movement, that all proceeds with equilibrium and the needed rhythm. It is said that all is then carried 'onward and upward and through' into further expansions of consciousness.

It was noticed that unlike 'onward' and 'upward', 'through' has no opposite. We are told that this word 'through' describes 'the next racial expansion of consciousness'. The Group together pondered the significance of this statement. What did it mean in terms of the work we were doing? And, if possible, what did it mean in the highest sense we could apprehend because that then would guide how we work.

A noticeable change was coming over the Group. Although we had always come together in esoteric discussion on what was emerging in consciousness, we were finding that we, as a single group entity, were drawing through thought or ideas and each one who spoke was speaking as representative of this emerging thought. This is somewhat difficult to describe in words but all members were in agreement that something new, something different, was happening. The Group had entered another phase of experience, of operation – a fifth phase of the Group.

August 2001

And so we arrived at a rather remarkable meeting in August 2001. Everybody noticed a depth of change not only from the previous meeting but also from all previous meetings. We were 'in another place'. We understood what was happening by comparison with how the meeting had operated in the past, and although there had often been new phases and changes this one was by far the most profound.

It was evident that every member in the Group was entirely focused within the group-entity consciousness and together researching the future that was emerging. Particular issues and aspects were brought to focus. There was a depth of silence behind it all that had never been known to this extent before, and a realisation that everyone was involved in this held point of tension. As it is said, the silence of the secret place settled upon the Group.

There was one point during that meeting when we all entered into actual silence for a space of some minutes, spontaneously and as one single entity. It was evident that everyone was responding to the sound, to that which was sounding, all immersed with rapt attention, together as a group – a single entity. An experience lived, recognised and understood by everyone. It was also obvious as we noticed the response to the sound of that which was emerging, that we were aware that we could not allow noise, that noise which invades a group when anyone breaks from the point of tension and begins to address personal matters or for one reason or another is following thought that separates from the group's focused intent.

Within this experience it dawns on the group consciousness that this is life-sharing. The Entity is a living entity and we are all sharing in and expressing through that life. This is the fifth phase of the Group. Gone is any necessity to rectify anything in the Group. Moving as a single entity we increasingly will experience identical at-one-ness, life-sharing. Another thing of which we are aware is that as we experience and therefore anchor the possibility of such sharing of life we are sounding the note of sharing (which is the keynote of Aquarius) and of right relationship, right through into human awareness.

So here we all were at a particular moment in August 2001. The group entity was very much in charge and the individuals as a unity were considering not only what was emerging, but also how the word *through* obviates the work we have to do; how this word *through* could be considered and defined and understood and expressed, and the Group was meditatively in discussion. It really had moved from anything that could possibly be called concrete mind. It moved within intuitive levels.

Through

We have grown in consciousness on this planet by living in and through form and in the process, having so identified with forms as our own true being, we seek a way to move *with our developed awareness* beyond the confining form nature. We note that it is within the field of time and space that human consciousness grows into its true divinity, expressed and directed. But how easily we can relate to the emotional states or mental fixations! Is it any wonder that we find ourselves exhibiting an uneven rhythm, out of kilter with life, as we live within the illusion of time? Humanity has moved so greatly within the material sense that it has lost the rhythm of the eternal, lost the rhythm of spirit, which we are recapturing on the path of return to the Father.

The resolution lies in that word *through*. It describes the next racial expansion of consciousness. Let us move onward and upward in Life; let us move in that space which is not form, which is between forms, even as we are not the forms, that is, within our own true dimension. Let us move *through*.

Those elements, if we may call them such – space or place and time – that provide the dimensions within which humanity grows to a full conscious awareness of divinity – are also illusions when identified with, when seen as that which is the only true world. How do we overcome this? We move *through* it. The problem is, we stop off along the way and get ourselves lost in it, indulge in it, play in it, work in it, grow in it and *through* it. But once we begin to address the next necessary phase in human consciousness, the monadic, which is still so far off generally speaking, then we have to see time and space as something that we use or not at will and that implies freedom from those elements that have guaranteed our possibility of achievement throughout the ages. Time to come home kids!

Through. Through what? Between? Throughout? The realisation that life permeates all, and if we identify with life as it permeates time and space then we are identified with life and not with time and space per se? That we may move with freedom within these dimensions? That we leave behind the friction of the world of form and move with the least possible effort, or expenditure of force? That we move within the rhythm of life?

On our journey in and through life we must move onward and upward and *through*. Onward to greater things, upward out of the material density of consciousness and through into unrestrained living expression. We do not look back. We cannot afford to waste time decrying this or that, or in regret, or concern over past error. This is a planet of 'experimentation' where what we find does not work we have the opportunity to leave it behind, and move on. Perhaps we do have things to repair but in the realisations of the movement onward those things dissipate from the lack of supportive energy.

We may look at the pairs of opposites. We must move onward, not backward. We must move upward, not downward. We must move *through* – but *through* has no opposite, which is quite a clue. For comparison, we may look at *through* as against 'around'. *Through* interpenetrates, permeates and transforms energy-wise. It assures the required or necessary changes. It demonstrates movement. 'Around' still implies there is something 'between'. There *is* nothing 'between' in the movement of *through*. 'Around' does not guarantee onward and upward movement as does *through*.

Through most definitely implies movement. There is nothing static in the universe. There is never a time when we will find there is no more to discover somewhere in the universe. Always it will be onward, upward and through. But we have come to a point in human evolution where *through* offers us a means for the next movement or expansion of consciousness. The way to do things? It seems so. Let us look at some examples or possibilities and discover the mode of its operation.

- *Through* what? Between the pairs of opposites? We think of the message of the Buddha and the noble middle path.

- We recall that St. Paul, in writing to the Jewish Christians, pointed to the fact that Christ passed *through* the curtain, that is of his own human nature, and opened the way in understanding for us also to pass in conscious awareness beyond the outer world of form and into the realm of our true being.

- We consider that when the Life aspect is entered in full conscious awareness then the second aspect is no longer required as an intermediate position in the scale of consciousness. It gives way. Then there is a direct flow *through* between the monad and the etheric, the true physical body of expression, the energy body, anchoring upon the outer plane of expression.

• When humanity really begins to express in terms of light and love and the will-to-good then the Christ can come and this will be inevitable because he cannot deny that which has invoked him. In this we understand invocation and evocation in operation and it is said that he is 'pulled *through*' into expression, and that the physical plane becomes his area of expression.

• We also understand that when certain members of the Hierarchy move onward to higher work, making vacancies all the way down the line, then others are required to move to fill the positions vacated. Again we have the sense that they are drawn onward, upward and *through*. All have a great opportunity to move and to serve at a higher stage of awareness, and with increased and intensified service.

• We all know the story of the woman who, seeking healing, reached out and touched the hem of Christ's garment. The Christ felt virtue leave him. There was no obstruction or hindrance to the free flow of healing energy that immediately moved *through* the Christ to the woman concerned. She received healing.

• When we read the New Testament story of the crucifixion of the Christ we are told that the veil of the Temple was rent in twain from the top to the bottom. Esoterically speaking, at that moment a rent was made in the etheric veil of the planet thus letting in the light, permitting a new type of illumination to pour *through* into the consciousness of humanity in a direct manner. Love could now begin to be understood and to express in a deeper sense than before.

We may see that, at an extreme point of tension and with unwavering intent, a great Son of God let in the light and made a great contribution to human consciousness. All the way through the story of Christ's life on earth we may penetrate to deeper meanings than were understood in the past age, and note examples of principle expressed which give guidance and instruction to those who serve in our time, not only to individual disciples but to the group entities as they function in the New Day in Aquarius.

So the Group at this stage, preoccupied with the work ahead and maintaining an unwavering and united point of tension, recognised the energies flowing into and *through* the Group and knew that the work could proceed rapidly and without hindrance.

Application into the work

We had considered much about that word *through* but what would happen if it were in operation in the events and circumstances of our group life and our individual lives? What may we expect to see if the required energies and influences flowed unimpeded through us into the many situations and challenges experienced by us and by those associated with us? And also into inter-group life?

We were aware that the flow of energies pouring through the Group and out into the world at large was of major concern as the new thinking leading into a new day made its presence felt out into the affairs of humanity as a whole. We understood our task as the direction of these energies and that of all groups involved with the growth of human consciousness, the task of the one world group of servers to which we all belong.

CHAPTER FIVE
Things Were Beginning to Happen

The group members decided to enter upon a project of experimentation with the movement and effects of the idea *through* as applied within our thinking, within our everyday lives and within our service activities. We recognised the possibilities of implementing required change, resolution, onward movement in and through situations and basically, observing just how the energies were set in motion or moved into expression as we understood and held the point of tension or focus in thought. We all agreed to compare notes and to share our insights and discoveries, some of which follow.

One group member spoke of 'sharing' and that it held a particular significance in the world of this moment. She commented:

"Sharing is so related to *through* – when we share we allow something to flow throughout the scope of the sharing. Ultimately we are sharing life, as everything we share is related to life and to that life more abundant. The abundance is in the extension through sharing – that is how we allow abundance to manifest – through sharing.

"Sharing is also automatic when we live oneness, when there are no barriers in one's nature. The sharing we see happening in the world is a symptom and a triumphant affirmation of the externalisation of the inner oneness. This comes from the heart of humanity through the 'ordinary' men and women who donate, give, share what they have – such as the donations to the humanitarian agencies and appeals. There is certainly a will to share – it needs only to be galvanised into global coordinated expression – into livingness.

"But sharing is applied to all dimensions – spiritual sharing, life sharing, is the natural state of being. We have just to realise it into outer expression."

The following are comments from a member of the Group who is in her 88th year and who nowadays attends meetings infrequently and yet is ever attuned to, and merged with, the group life and awareness:

"For so long I have served with this Group and have entered an experience of Oneness that I can only describe as 'divine ecstasy'. The door was opened by the group life and together we walked *through*. I know a freedom not known before. It is freedom from fear, freedom from confinement, but more than that, it is the freedom of life itself. It redefines many things, outlooks, attitudes and understanding in general.

"Earlier approaches are made trivial in my sight. We may think about contacting a previous incarnation or 'event' but once living and expressing within a state of oneness, all past lives appear as just one and the same life we have been experiencing.

"Recently I was in my chemist's shop and in the flash of a moment I '*became* the chemist' and could see everything in the shop through his eyes. It was a startling experience demonstrating to me just how at-one everyone is."

A third group member spoke of continuing experiences of synchronicity in thought between herself and others on her team in the world of business:

"Explaining this, trying to write it down, is like meshing words together to describe something that is 'experienced' and the true meaning is found in being immersed in this state – not in the words that only end up putting boundaries and artificial form and structure around it.

"When we operate with a sense of *through*, we do not view things serially. When knowledge is passed on (like from generation to generation; from teacher to student; from boss to subordinate – in fact the whole learning experience as we know it now), then time is indeed serially experienced. We can only learn the next thing after we have learnt the current thing – because there is a sequence. We need to know 'this' before we can learn 'that'.

"But our consciousnesses work together (as part of a group consciousness) and through permeation of our energies and being (osmosis?), then all just 'is'. We are in synch; sharing awareness; interconnected – then we have access to all. It is instant, as the knowledge is not passed down or along in a 'serial time fashion'. It is there to access through our consciousness and awareness, blending to the shared common purpose.

"'Seriality' has no meaning because it is all there for us to merge, blend, permeate and use as required – as a group fusion of purpose – not for individual purpose."

Another co-worker told of the following experience:

"Recently I was involved in a photoshoot and when afterwards I reflected on the day it seemed there were elements of *through* in operation.

"In hindsight it was astonishing to realise that although none of the people involved had worked together before, they lost no time with the usual 'getting to know each other' pleasantries and immediately attended to fulfilling their role in the task in hand.

"The make-up artist barely said hello before wanting to locate the nearest power point for the hot-rollers. After a brief confirmation of the 'look' we were going for, she proceeded quietly with make-up and hair for the next two hours.

"At the studio the actor changed into costume, final adjustments were made to hair and make-up, while I briefed the photographer, and then it began...

"I had anticipated that we would need the whole day to take the series of photographs which required changes of make-up, hair, wardrobe, lighting, etc. However, the assembled team quickly adopted a rhythm that was characterised by:

- a creative tension (i.e. taut focus on purpose freely including all participants' creative energy)

- a quietness on the set (devoid of any extraneous conversation other than that related to achieving the purpose)

- an obliviousness to time (whilst at the same time working quickly but without any sense of pressure or even any awareness of time)

- a sense of economy (we knew we had the right shot without straining the resources with overshooting and multiple variations. Also I was aware that when we had the shot there was an energy shift which marked completion)

"It would be a mistake to assume that the quietness on the set was devoid of joy, laughter and a sense of fun – these qualities were present. However, the 'noise' that happens when individuals are preoccupied with matters other than the task at hand – either by word, thought or deed – was absent. All participants were fully present and focused on the task at hand. And we finished two hours early!!

"Afterwards in explaining to a friend the feeling on the shoot I said there was a sense of 'ease' or 'effortlessness' about the day which results from holding the point of tension. Only an *apparent* paradox. We could say that all involved did a professional job and indeed they did. But that doesn't exactly encapsulate the experience on the day which was more than mere professionalism – it was beyond that – a quiet focused taut team rhythmically and effectively performed a task as if they had all worked together for years."

An actor speaking to one of the group members shared the following:

"Regardless of what they may say, it's not until you're working with another actor that you know in a moment their motivation for wanting to act. It is present, beyond the scene you're doing. You sense it immediately – everything revealed in a moment. And if you are truly open then an intimate exchange may take place through the work where you 'merge' with the other person. It's related to understanding them deeply and, consequently, you feel like you take a bit of them with you forever, and you suspect they do likewise."

Another group member shared the following account:

"In one of my classes there was a senior student who had always been 'difficult'. She had been highly reactive, hypersensitive and frequently confrontational. I had allowed things to limp along for some time, mainly concerned with containing the situation so that it did not disrupt the learning for everyone else. One lesson however, I ran out of patience, having sorely tired of her rudeness and borderline abuse. There was a direct confrontation in which I asked her to leave and not return until she could be polite. I subsequently referred the matter to my senior who undertook to support me with a mediated resolution. Unfortunately the 'mediation' that followed did not go well, resulting in the student attacking me in a vindictive and personal way. While I felt disempowered and upset by this, at least the student had been put on notice that if she chose to return to class it was on the condition that she caused no further disruption. Also, at the student's request, I agreed not to discuss any of her work unless she asked for feedback.

"The mediation and subsequent pseudo-resolution disturbed me and I discussed this with a co-worker, seeking support and a more constructive perspective. She assured me that there would be 'a way *through*' the situation and we resolved to hold that thought in focus.

"The first lesson the student returned to class I felt some trepidation. As I stood at the front of the room and began the lesson I made eye contact with each of the students. I was aware of a feeling of hostility and a confrontational stare from this student and as I looked at her I experienced initially anxiety and stress, but then over the top of this another feeling swept in. It felt as though there was a powerful but subtle exchange between us in which loving energy was drawn forth from my heart centre. I was aware of all stress dissipating, of all expectations dissolving, and of a feeling of loving impartiality towards her. I maintained this attitude and in so doing the situation seemed diffused. The student seemed affected too, her stare ceased and she just blended into the class, hostility apparently forgotten.

"Over the weeks I continued to operate with the same loving attitude and respected her request for 'space'. On one occasion she appeared to bait me, however I just looked her directly and silently in the eyes, and she quietened. Gradually, she began to approach me for help with her work and while there was never a sense of closeness or friendship between us, there was a more respectful working relationship free of aggravation."

And the story unfolded further:

"After the last group meeting I had been thinking about *throughness* as a process and even an attitude with which to approach things/situations/people. Perhaps a 'modus operandi', keeping in mind the idea of 'rhythm' and the 'least possible effort', not as a tactic but as *a way through*.

"My school is rich with opportunities to apply such an approach...

"Recently there has been a lot of conflict in the school among the staff over the implementation of a new assessment and reporting system as a result of a new curriculum.

"A few weeks ago we had a staff meeting that was particularly fractious at which an administrator handled things in a way which allowed for me to be attacked by a very vocal, negative minority resisting change. The issues discussed were subsequently 'resolved' by unsatisfactory compromise.

"A couple of weeks after this we had another staff meeting at which we were to discuss another potentially inflammatory issue. Initially, the relieving principal planned to lead the discussion after which I would facilitate some kind of vote-type finish. However, at short notice she decided she would go to the Student Forum on the same issue instead. After this piece of delegation by abdication, I was then left to negotiate with the second in charge. At that point, I decided to 'do it myself'. That weekend I focused on the notion of *a way through* and held that thought.

"Come the Monday meeting, I introduced the issues and facilitated the discussion as planned, all the while being aware of having no agenda, of not controlling the discussion, of allowing all of us to find a way *through*. I became aware of a descending calm in the room, of a 'space' opening up, of a freeing up of energy. People spoke freely, there were silences, there was no argument or debate in which one tried to make another agree, everyone's contributions were accepted as equal, and some people spoke who rarely do. After the meeting several people came to me to comment on how calm it had been.

"I was amazed and delighted by what seemed to be the transformation of our staff. I had never experienced such an amiable, peaceful meeting at our school. It gave me hope that we can be a harmoniously interactive staff and it confirmed to me that transformation can be immediate and significant."

And here is another contribution:

"The way I see this Group working…

"There are moments of silence and stillness within the Group which *allow in* a certain energy and which facilitates the group 'flow'. This way of group functioning draws forth the individual into the whole and through the interaction of the members is woven a kind of fabric – the fabric of consciousness, an expression of the new.

"I see implications in this for the way I work in an education setting. I am aware of another possibility for leadership that seems more inclusive (i.e. everyone being the leader together) that involves *allowing in* the energy for change such that the staff group themselves bring the change into manifestation in the way that is right for them.

"This is contrary to the leadership I see around me both in theory and practice in that it does not involve one or a small group of people having a 'vision', which is then used to inspire others who then come 'on board' (for the ride!). It does not require convincing others, or getting others to agree to something. It actually requires the 'opening up' of a space, a silence, a stillness, into which can flow an energy that is non-threatening, that promises to 'hear' everyone and that allows creativity to emerge from lots of people.

"I am aware that to facilitate such a process I can have no thought for my own self in this and not a care for my reputation or whatever, and this is where I see others fall into an unproductive process of leadership. There needs to be nothing at stake and especially no agenda or preconceived expectations of outcomes."

Another co-worker was surprised to notice the exceptionally free flow of thought between group members, even telepathically registered, and made the following observation:

"As I spoke with a co-worker and made a particular comment I was aware in a flash of the response from her mind and that we were both aware of this immediate communication. We laughed together as we compared our thought about the spontaneity of the happening.

"It occurred to me that in a group that leaves behind personal emphasis and identifications, thought moves freely and is known to each and all. Then *through*-ness exists – there is a free flow *through* and between all – no need, no impulse, to erect protective barriers as do separated personalities. This is a soul group, a group soul, in operation."

Another shared an experience of 'simultaneous awareness':

"Sitting quietly in the kitchen, contemplating my work at the table, immersed in thought. Children playing together, coming over, asking questions, exchanging a few words, including me in their games. I'm in both – my thoughts, their games ... our voices; blending like instruments in a piece of musical harmony. My consciousness seems expanded while I exist within two states of being – one inner, one outer. I experience simultaneous awareness and all seems at peace in a state of perfect balance. I speculate on the development of human consciousness as an expansive one in which we act consciously within the world and exist consciously within a state of being."

And finally, another's experience:

"Over the past few months I have been contacting different people at the moment that they were about to contact me – this has occurred a couple of times a week. This elicited such comments as 'You're a mind reader', 'I can't believe it, I just had your business card out ready to call you', 'You must have been reading my thoughts – I was just about to call you' and so on. This has happened with people that I have worked with over the years and hence know well but also with people that I have never met and only talked to on the phone a few times. So it is not just the case that when you get to know someone so well, you can think as one or be in tune with them – it happens with 'strangers'.

"It is not a case of telepathy or reading someone's mind because it is not as proactive or 'projective' as that. It is an awareness of things that have to be done when working on projects and the awareness of people involved in this work. Working jointly on activities, you are in the same space so to speak, and therefore communication seems to be by infusion (though this is not the best word to describe it – immersion in the same space therefore a permeation of thought which provides direct access to knowledge). When you are in this space (even for a split moment) things don't seem to work sequentially – i.e. you think of me and hence this triggers me to think of you and pick up the phone. It happens at the *same time*, or so it seems. That is why time is an illusion as we think that we have to have cause and effect rather than being in the same space and 'sharing' knowledge."

* * * * *

As the Group began to focus thought within the significance of that idea *through* we discovered it in operation within our everyday lives. But more importantly there was the realisation of its vaster significance within the greater scheme of things, its function in the movement onward in the consciousness of the human race.

* * * * *

Snippets from A Group Conversation on *Through*

Breakthrough

"May we think of *through* in terms of 'breakthrough'? I am reminded of that story of the crucifixion and that the veil of the temple was rent in twain. We considered the fact that Christ passed *through* the curtain of his own human nature and opened the way before us. But also as Head of Hierarchy he rent the veil which hid Hierarchy from the sight of the human kingdom, symbolically speaking. He made it possible for easier contact to be made between humanity and Hierarchy.

"Can we see a service, a contribution, to the work of our time, to the next phase of conscious communication, in breaking *through* that seemingly impenetrable reality of time, space, distance, that deceives our consciousness, and into a much more rapid, clearer communication with Hierarchy or the spiritual kingdom, one which is not confused or separated by the world of forms? As individuals and as a group may we open the way forward for humanity, following Christ's example?"

Entering

"Another thought that occurs is that we are considering an expansion of consciousness as we enter a new and greater dimension so that we are no longer separate from it. At the same time *as we enter into* these worlds we find their energies *entering into us*, becoming a driving force in our lives. We may well understand how necessary it is to stand at the centre of our being otherwise there will be the danger of personality stimulation and the risk of disruption and misuse of the energies contacted."

The Eye of the Needle

"Another angle is that it is impossible to go *through* and cart a whole heap of rubbish with us. This is the actuality. It is an aspect of the 'eye of the needle' story. Said Christ: 'It is easier for a camel to go through the eye of a needle than for a rich man to enter the kingdom of heaven.'

"Some Old Testament exponents have thought this allusion is historical fact. It is said there was a gate that led into Jerusalem that was too low to allow a loaded camel through and the camel had to be unloaded to pass into the city. The gate was called 'the Eye of the Needle'.

"So we cannot carry our burdens through the gates. In other words, there's no point in trying to embrace this task if you're going to keep carting this baggage with you. We may be ever so willing to work in this way, recognise it as the next step, but still be stuck with all those things that prevent that next step, inhibiting breakthrough."

Moving on

"And we cannot hang back because others may want us to stay back with them. We must move on and so leave a line of light. No one ever served a planet by being convinced that they had to stay back and not move because others were not ready. *Through* reveals this principle. Christ moved *through* the curtain of his own human nature. Unless we move *through* to our own true being we are not serving by opening the way *through* to the next expansion of consciousness for the race."

The Heart

"Our motivation is on behalf of the human race. We work from the heart – from the centre of life and love. We recognise that circulation of the 'life more abundantly' proceeding out from the heart of Life itself, beating at the very centre of the universe. And we know our role to be distributors of Life and not so much recipients."

There are a few teachers in the Group and the following thought was evoked during this conversation:

Education

"Thinking about education in our schools and universities, it seems our discussion could be most applicable to the changes many recognise are needed in our education system today. How may we consider this word *through* in this regard? Are we looking at *drawing through*? We may touch that point in others that they also find themselves speaking with us from that centre.

"In recent times we have searched out truer approaches to education and its true meaning. We have pointed to the Latin *educare*, to lead out. In the time we are entering it may be more a matter of 'drawing out' or 'through' than 'leading out' – *through* from our centre – from their centre – a touching at *the* centre. There is a realisation of the magnetic in the process."

Forces

"*Through* brings the best solution and allows life to express regardless of apparent obstruction or the forces which would restrain or restrict onward movement for the good of the whole. Let us note that we cannot assist if we are projecting those same forces."

"When things appear magically to come together and flow, we note that we could not have planned a better outcome even with the best of thought. As inner sight (realisation) develops (clears) we will note the source, the origin, and note how energies and forces move *through* into expression from the poised centre of loving will or intention."

Energy

"*Through* compels us to perceive in terms of energy and to focus on that which pervades form."

Radioactivity

"May we liken *through* to radioactivity which is said to 'go through everything' just like radio waves?"

Understanding the Operation of Through

"How does *through* move into operation? Rather than engaging in a mental search let us experiment with it intuitively, in life expression and experience. We need to employ it and we may then define its operation as we see it working out in our own experience."

Finally someone reminded us of the statement:

"Revelation flows *through* me, I know it not."

We may continue to find many examples of the significance of that word *through* in operation. It expresses the rhythm of life; it demonstrates the absence of force, the way of energy flow. It can express in every field of human endeavour without exception. When people focus in, work from, the centre of their being there is a free flow soul to soul between them. The same is true of groups. There can be a free exchange between groups anywhere in the world. It is the basis of true understanding and cooperative endeavour.

Chapter six
Across the World

On the opposite side of the planet another group was entering into similar experiences to those that we were currently researching. There had been an ongoing sharing of thought between the groups as we all considered the significance of that word *through*.

The following ongoing e-mail exchanges reveal another example of this unfolding experience:

Co-worker: "We face quite a challenge here at this time. Not only are there 'turf' issues, with many individuals and groups in our outreach work looking at their own needs first instead of all needs being met when the greater good is the shared focus, but we ourselves are facing the fact that we cannot agree on where we are going and how to get there. There has to be a way to handle or facilitate this disruption to the work that is at once inclusive and moves us *through*. What do you think?"

Author: "It is difficult to move through these situations when the emphasis or the focus is primarily on the forms of expression and the essential unity is overlooked.

"A co-worker from a country centre just called and discussed her local happenings with all the challenges which they can present to a concerned member of a community and of humanity itself. We considered the process of *through* and how it operates. It is so different from past and personal ways.

"I realise that I consider *through* mainly as it operates through and within the dimension of our being that we call spiritual or subjective, and of course this is where it arises and from whence it directs and enlivens every aspect of our expression right out into physical plane living. It is and must be transformative, progressive, life-giving in its effect.

"If we stand centred and observe the usual 'battles' where people disagree over many issues, we can identify that the sticking point, or the failure to find a solution, is due to the fact that those involved have a personal stake in the matter. Until our only motivation is the good of the whole, until our decisions are made on the long term view to the benefit of the planet and future generations, and until we see ourselves only as instruments to bring about this desirable outcome, we are not really working for, fighting for, human progress (onward, upward and through) but are getting the image of our personal selves and their opinions in the way.

"Said my country co-worker: 'But this is not easy!' Neither is it usual but it is imperative to understand and to implement if we would take this next step in human consciousness."

Co-worker: "A breakthrough has occurred since last we were in touch! Holding the focus on *through* (essential unity), moving through, a way through, at every turn when an apparent road block – attitude, opinion, hopelessness, whatever – would either stop process or cause irritation in the system, by speaking the language of *through* and inclusiveness and possibility (with no personal agenda) virtually everyone found a way to 'think bigger', to mind stretch a bit, and we walked through a potentially difficult and explosive situation in a way that serves the entire community, with a focus on the future and what will best serve the common good.

"As we discussed earlier, and is now visible in operation, *through* does not have an opposite, and implies moving past (*through*) duality to a truer expression of oneness which always exists yet seems elusive at times when we are focused in separative ways (thinking, feeling, acting). Youth demonstrate a capacity to immediately grab the concept of *through* – creating from that place within them, and it's not about form. This is excellent, and a practical application of a number of principles and the fact that *through* holds the key to the next expansion of consciousness of the race which is inevitably tied to the revelation of oneness."

Author: "As we research *through* as it 'describes the next racial expansion of consciousness' we are finding it in operation and revealing itself to us. Not all are seeing its process and results to the degree that you are in the fertile field of your work in community and in group. If it holds the 'next expansion' and we find it moves immediately into operation as we cooperate with its principle, then we can assume that 'its time has fully come' and we must be its exponents."

Co-worker: "Meanwhile, back at the ranch, there is extreme discomfort as there is an insistence to focus on the form and formalities of form to the exclusion of the realisation of oneness. It does not seem possible to move *through* in our present group formation, and perhaps that is just as well. With the Pluto-Saturn opposition it is apparent that a re-defining of groups is necessary and the old forms simply cannot withstand the pressure and must transform, which of course we experience as destruction right out here. Pluto takes us deep into our belief system, exposing all, and Saturn places a pressure on the form itself as it must conform to the sphere of influence and responsibility."

Author: "We can make the mistake of protecting forms that no longer serve, feeling the necessity to hold them to the original vision. This may result in an attempt to retrieve an impossible situation and try to make it work. We need insight and the understanding of right timing – when to relinquish and move on."

Co-worker: "This re-defining of groups is quite something and isn't it incredible how many groups are experiencing the splitting up and rearranging of personnel at this moment in time? Immediately for us and others it has become apparent that there is the emerging of a group around energy or consciousness rather than the development of a group around a form or specific project. This emergent reality is consistent with how your group has worked over these many years and demonstrates a spiritual principle. As the group formed as a direct result of sounding the note, projects and activities were attracted to and through the group – not vice-versa.

"As we hear from other groups who are experiencing similar challenges, in some cases the work is simply split into two, as many seek to follow a particular line which seems to delineate as either inward focused or outward focused. We are all challenged to acknowledge that both types of groups are required within the whole of expression of that great unity which is the one work. There are those who serve the needs of the more objective or external side of the work and the general public, and then there are those whose service is principally concerned with the subjective realities and their manifestation into outer expression. And yet both types of groups require their subjective anchorage and their external expression. The difference appears only in their major area of focus in the work. And thus are all areas of the work covered.

" In this time of Aquarius it seems necessary to follow the line of inclusiveness, of Oneness, of the realisation of the inner and outer simultaneous reality."

Author: "The New Group of World Servers is a great world group subjectively linked and without outer organisation. It could be said that our Group is understanding and expressing an externalisation of the New Group of World Servers – what it looks like in externalisation. And this does not mean organisation. It is an externalisation of conscious realisation. We work loosely with other groups out here. We do not see the necessity to build great external networks. We understand the subjective reality to such a degree that *that* consciously permeates the outer work and the outer understanding of relationship between group workers without the necessity of organisation.

"But what is externalising is that very awareness. What is externalising is the true conscious awareness of that great group, into outer consciousness. They are already a unified group in incarnation requiring no further organisation. This is the only way a great subjective group can externalise."

Co-worker: "With the community it did move through into a new day or way of expression, whereas resolution was achieved in the other group, as with many, by agreement to move in different directions within the work."

* * * * *

The principles involved apply equally to international affairs as to personal, group and inter-group issues and movement. The urgent responsibility to hold the united point of tension within the world group at this critical moment in world affairs, and without wavering or movement off-centre, is understood completely by all working consciously within that greater group on behalf of the forward movement of human consciousness and affairs. So is the way open for the inflow of new and vital energies needed in the world of today for resolution, for new vision, for inspiration, for the clarity to identify the nature of all the issues involved that can lead to separative attitudes. This inflow allows for the recognition of the basic oneness of the human race as a whole, the direction of the relevant energies of revelation, *through* the crisis of opportunity, to resolution, and into the reorganisation of world thought and the building of the new civilisation according to divine plan and purpose.

CHAPTER SEVEN
Oneness to Synthesis

Do we really believe we know what Oneness is in actuality? Oneness is that essential unity which underlies the whole of creation. It is non-separateness, a universal inclusiveness. The only true way Oneness may be revealed is as it is seen expressing through the life of one who knows and demonstrates its nature by conscious participation in this basic unity.

We stand at a time when we as a human race have created myriad forms through which we express our intention, our understanding and our purpose. Humanity has a great tenacity to hold on to whatever it creates. Anything that becomes an established organisation or a form of teaching is in danger of believing it owns a superior philosophy or an exclusive correctness which then can exclude the creative formulas or organisation of others or impose its viewpoint upon others. It is the basis of disagreement, conflict and oppression.

Along came the reformists who resisted oppression and demanded freedom to express within a different set of forms. Although this was a step in the right direction, a breaking free from a particular tyranny, it was only addressing the problem in the same dimension – within the world of form – a moving of things around in the plane of effects and without reference to or understanding of the deeper realm of cause. It invariably led to further conflict. And yet humanity continued to learn through the experience as it always does.

With clearer vision we understand that rather than *reformation* the answer lies in *transformation* – the movement across to another dimension of being – the recognition of the spiritual quality that informs and enlightens the form.

Unless we can capture the vision that is behind and emerging *through* any form of expression we still remain a prisoner of form. Do we see any of the writings, teachings or groups to which we may respond or subscribe as revealing that which is entirely other than themselves? What is not usually understood is that reality not only exists apart from the form but so far beyond it that the written or spoken word is no more than an approximation of something that is beyond confinement in any such form. In a similar sense we may express reality through many forms of expression, including our life expression, and to our degree of realisation it approximates the reality. At the same time it remains concealed from the many who focus upon its form.

In our prodigal journey we have forgotten. We have not created oneness. It exists. We have forgotten. But we have created forms. We have been very good at it, abundantly so! But if we ever feel we have 'the last word', that everything is based in that or revolves around it, that there is nothing more to add, then we have closed the door on further enlightenment and added to the belief in separation. As we enter the new era the inclusive nature of the energies of Aquarius show up the situation in sharp relief.

What is needed? We see the response to the recognised need of the present time already in operation all around the world. Individuals merge and work in groups for the human family, for the planet and its environment and for the greater scheme of things.

There follows the recognition that the world groups are part of *one great movement*. Each group is responsible for some piece or aspect of the work as a whole. Some groups may come together at times in a cooperative project or in conference but it is the realisation of the *unity of intention* and not of the forms that is required to make a transformative impact into human consciousness. It is as the world groups together reveal this essential unity behind the world of forms that they guarantee the movement forward of the human consciousness as a whole.

In other words, we need to be demonstrating our internal unity, our understanding of the nature of Oneness, and not perpetuate past error in emphasis upon the form side, believing it useful or even wise to pressure the group forms together or to canvass for numbers to fill out any group form. When group principles are truly understood and in operation a group will attract, will draw to itself by its very radiatory life expression, all those workers whose task lies within that group, and they then work together with the group members already involved.

If we observe life, events and our work from the inner side then we have a clear picture freed from the obscuring nature of forms, including those of the concrete mind, that can convince us of the rectitude of our external assessments and decisions. In a more obvious scenario we may see those engaged in programs for human betterment and aid working selflessly, often in dire circumstances, and without thought for anything other than the demands of the task before them. On the other hand we may observe vested interests holding great monopolies in world trade and commodities, even to the basic necessities of life, building massive forms and structures for profit while they shut their eyes to the suffering of the great numbers of humanity without sufficient food, shelter, medicines and all that is basic to human development and dignity.

This may seem an extreme comparison but spiritual groups themselves may not be free from this very same pattern if they believe they have the best or only way. They can be equally as guilty of creating this separative attitude as are the monopolies of the vested interests who deprive humanity of material sustenance. These groups deprive humanity of spiritual sustenance.

It is not unknown that a person, an organisation or a group may believe they have a *monopoly on truth* or the best way – the best way for some yes, if it is natural to them. But can we see the many ways as serving the many types and that the *inner unity* reflects into the outer group expression? It is in actuality the supportive energy which we all experience as we work together for the progress of the work of the world.

It pays us to check the nature of the forces that are constantly being emitted from our group. Are they promoting that essential unity imperative to the resolution of world problems so identifiable as stemming from separative beliefs and attitudes? Or are they reinforcing or stimulating the separative forces already rampant across the planet? Are we a part of the solution *in energy* as well as in activity? A sobering thought!

Wherever we may find individuals within a group fighting for an individual viewpoint to be accepted and instituted by the others in the group and generally holding back onward movement and response to a world in the process of vast change, then we are challenged to assess the forces let loose. It may not be noticed that such forces emitted by a group may be of a similar vibration to the far more obvious aggression intensifying in the world of today and before us daily on our television screens.

These forces emitted by a group can add to the forces of aggression even though the group may feel it is working for the good of the world whole. This problem exists where a group or individuals in a group have not yet moved from the personal focus into that of the soul or true group understanding. This recognition should encourage all of us to submerge the personal in favour of the soul expression of the group. It can be a particularly difficult and blind stage for any group.

The fact is that unless we are expressing the pure essence of Oneness in and through our group life and work we may still be adding to those old persuasive thought forms from a past age or we may be in danger of materialising or distorting the Aquarian vision along with its themes of soul or group awareness, oneness, freedom and service to the world and its humanity.

Thoughts from a group member

"As we can all observe the same things and the same breadth and scope of life then we are all observing from the same point. We are one at that point that is not of the manifesting world but operates through it and observes it unfolding. It is interesting how TV and the media assist us to all be at the same point of observation.

"When we focus *as a group* on the emerging realisations we are taking up that point of oneness and are experiencing oneness. We have then only to realise it and live it through the world.

"I have been testing this out for some time without realising that was what I was doing. When I watch my personality reacting to something and realise that I am just observing it as something external to the observing point of light I am, the reaction falls away and no longer touches the realised 'centre' of being. It's like shrugging off a too tightly fitting coat!

"Watching the world leaders and nations going through the same process in their own sphere of operation is very interesting. The reactive begins to become responsive to something else, something more, which renders the lesser identification irrelevant. It is an inspiring point of shift that is rippling through the world at the moment as we realise that we are all at the heart of the matter – the one heart, the human heart and the heart of the centre of our system.

"We are all hubs in the internet of human consciousness which is yet the one hub of life. All the manifesting world flows out from there, taking form and dissolving and taking new forms – yet we remain there at the centre of life, eternally there when all has come and gone, directing the ordered outflow that expresses Being in Matter."

What is Synthesis?

Can you imagine our world when the reality of Oneness is understood and expresses in a synthesis of endeavour towards the advancement of humankind, of all peoples and nations and indeed of all forms of life on the planet? Can you imagine what possible revelation may then dawn on our sight?

Wherever we find movements to bring unity and understanding, to bridge apparent gaps, to restore right human relationship, there we see the living energies of Oneness and Synthesis beginning to express.

But until we recognise the oneness that underlies all forms, basically that oneness that sees no separation and that knows there are no divisions in spiritual existence, we will not truly understand the nature of Synthesis, of the first aspect of divinity from which will emerge the new approach to God and the new civilisation.

What is Synthesis? It is never diminished; it contains all within it. It is beyond differentiation yet it is that great unity which incorporates every part, which is behind the creation of every part. It is the One and the many. It is Life itself.

As we stand at the beginning of a new time of emergence on our planet we understand that we have the responsibility to apprehend and bring into form that which life seeks to express in order to further the evolutionary growth of the human race as we move into Aquarius with all its newly contacted influences and energies.

When we approach the task from the recognition of synthesis, of the life aspect, we find we are focused within that undifferentiated area. It is complete, it is a whole, and we realise that it is only as there is a necessity for that next recognition to descend into expression that division or differentiation takes place. It is not a matter of 'going in there' and taking hold of something that Life may now wish to express. We cannot say 'Oh there it is, let's take that bit.' It is only as we understand that spirit informs matter from the planes of synthesis, from the formless worlds, that we understand our task (under such inspiration) to create the new forms or change present forms into more adequate forms to convey or approximate Life's intention for the next evolutionary movement, the expression of the new life in a new day.

It is important that we present a new outline, formulate 'change-statements', so that people are not held by the past ways, so they can begin to see where the onward movement is taking us, freeing the group from where it arrived at the end of the Piscean era so that it can begin to embrace those newer ideas and word forms and all those things which will convey the new moment. Life demands it.

Even disciples do not generally understand Synthesis. We have all been busy applying ourselves to the development of the intuition. The new race, already appearing among us, will be more responsive to the newer thought. They are naturally intuitive. The challenge for them is responsiveness to the next higher expression, the spiritual will. This is where we are heading and the members of the new race will no doubt be a part of that movement leading into this new time.

Let us give thought to cultivating an understanding of Oneness, Synthesis and Being.

* * * * *

Remember: Oneness is never followed by the word 'except' and Being has no otherwise.

CHAPTER EIGHT
Movement in Identical At-one-ness

It is quite a challenge to put words to the experience of identical at-one-ness without robbing it of its depth or even doing it an injustice. However let us proceed. As in the first book *Journey of a Lifetime* it may be useful to present a picture by way of an ongoing discussion between two co-workers.

Author: "What is emerging is emerging. We may think 'it is still in there' but only because we have to find adequate ways and words to define it – talk it into being, into expression, into objectivity. It is in fact already here. It has captured our total attention and it will influence our way of working, of seeing, of knowing. It can never be said that it is in any way exclusive to any group – it is emerging into human consciousness but must be apprehended by the group or groups. As we talk together about this newly emerging phase and its nature, we are assisting it into expression – it is the work we are doing. There is no doubt it is impinging upon group awareness everywhere and will be interpreted according to type and area of working.

"I also notice the effect – or actuality – that we are 'somewhere else' all the time even while fully present at some anchorage on the physical plane. This realisation continues to grow in clarity as we work together because we are always essentially together and in every subtle sense. This next phase is not only in need of definition but also needs to be anchored."

Co-worker: "Yes. It is as though I am somewhere else also even while fully present here. And I am aware of the thread that runs through everything. When we are in rhythm with the undulating flow from the inner to the outer planes time virtually disappears. We meet the moment, the need, even the demand and yet there is no stress – we move with the inner river that moves through everything or moves everything through."

Author: "Here we are, finding terms to define the experience. One should never need to define experience – it is defined in our very own awareness with all its subtleties, its shades, intensities and qualities. However, we seek to share the experience with others – to open the door if possible to a way through. The 'door'? The door is not a door. There is no door. There is only that obscuring veil composed of all our beliefs in separate states of existence, which may seem real enough on the outer level of our lives but which have no existence in the subtle and true realm of our being. We have said all this over and over in one way or another, through one topic or another. Where to go?"

Co-worker: "Earlier we saw how life-sharing worked through our respective areas of group function and work on either side of the planet. At particular moments we were aware of shared presence, singleness of being, and extra impetus of energy. But the realisation has moved now into the awareness, the state, the experience, that is a constant. It is unchanging. It is an awareness of identification, of life-sharing, that is present in every moment. It is not something we call upon. It is ever present. Or we are ever present within it."

Author: "It is that which stands on the edge of human consciousness at this time and invites participation. It presumes we already have clarity of thought and freedom of expression. It is a realisation of great freedom – the freedom of being – that which we truly are. We understand it signals a movement from the soul aspect into the life aspect. It is with such understanding that we approach the work of the future.

"Our experience has deepened. We recognise the capacity to identify together, consciously, within a state of being. It makes no difference where we are in the outward sense. The realisation of togetherness in every dimension, in thought and in the work is inevitable. It is not just known as a possibility. It is experienced.

"This can also happen with a group entity. The Group *has become* an entity. Just as the soul on its own plane is already an initiate of all degrees, we are all in process of becoming in actual expression what we are in essence. In that sense we *become* this. We *are* this but are using the word 'become' in the sense of *conscious realisation* of it. A group can become a 'single entity' in the same sense. So identification moves on, not just between two people, but also among all in the group and then progressively between groups. This is dependent upon the understanding that the whole group is a subjective unity without division in consciousness. There is nothing standardising in this recognition. It assures the freedom of expression of all groups on the outer plane while it reveals the source of their life and strength as together they work out planetary purpose according to their moment in time.

"We are recognising a state of Being within which we live and we move onward to a *conscious participation* within it. We have not created it – it has always existed. We have become aware of it and aware that we cannot exist apart from it. Those who do not understand the true nature of freedom may feel that something is about to be imposed upon them or taken from them. 'Where is my freedom if you take my will? No one is going to take my will.' Christ revealed the lesser will is superseded as it is merged with the greater Will. What has anyone lost when moving to a greater expression if divine purpose guides rather than personal reasons, purpose and desire?"

Co-worker: "We discussed identical at-one-ness in *Journey of a Lifetime* and now we are recognising a movement within this realisation, a deepening, a greater understanding, not only of the experience itself but its effects as we work out in the world. It has its own radiatory quality. Even if we look at just two people experiencing identical at-one-ness with one another there is nowhere that either starts or finishes. It is a complete unity. No divisions. One would never consider dividing one's own individualised being into separate parts, sections or segments, and similarly as we experience identical at-one-ness why would we ever think to separate this one being into two, or parts? And still each retains their individuality of expression, and together become more intensely and expressively themselves.

"There is an experience of complete freedom, complete movement. It is freedom from the lower planes of expression. It has an effect throughout our own living, throughout our environment, throughout our group. It has an effect as we work with other groups and we might share the experience of one such event that took place when I visited your city."

Author: "When the two of us were making a presentation at the meeting place of another group, we were aware that connectivity and receptivity was immediate and continued throughout the afternoon. It announced that we are all a part of the movement in the one work and the one world group. The effect was a free-flow through and between everyone and everyone's particular mode of service – it is all one work. Some of those gathered in that room commented on the unity expressing. In such an experience there is the recognition that we are all workers and we are all together in that meeting room and we all have various areas of expression in service in the outer world. We have always been together. We branch out into whatever is ours to do but are we not companions on the Way? Have we not always been? 'We're back! Haven't seen you for ages but have we ever been apart?' It is touching on a point of identification. The sharing of thought and ideas is an aspect of the greater sharing of life."

Co-worker: "So we describe an experience of identical at-one-ness, of shared presence in a presentation mode. An awareness of being the same being presenting, as though the in-breath and out-breath were one instead of two. No hesitation to pick up or put down a thought or word, carrying an idea from one to the other, between us."

Author: "Completely coordinated without effort or pre-arrangement. And even interesting to watch the very nature of it organise the field within which it would express."

Co-worker: "And no matter what the question or comment from the group, after some presentation by the two, the participants stood within that field, the life of the moment, and people began to realise that."

Author: "We actually were an entire group researching together, realising together. And it was obvious. One could feel that essence flowing through the whole room and the company there."

Co-worker: "Right through to a point of questions about programs in form. We had been speaking about the subjective, inner life and then there was an awareness of the inner to outer activity – it is all one – and that this group, as a group, was helping to support the outer activity from a subjective stance."

Author: "And the realisation that whoever was present, representative of various groups, we were all a unity in the work as a whole and within that we moved as one. That element that was there, shared by the two, that life-sharing experience, moved through the group. It incorporated the group as a whole and what the group experienced was life-sharing in whatever way they endeavoured to define it in comment at the end. It seemed a new experience for some people and one that appeared to be quite elevating.

"This is just one single example of life-sharing or identical at-one-ness recognised, lived between two people, moving out in their work together, incorporating every last person in that particular moment, in that particular piece of work, experienced together. This is one example but is there anywhere these two may move that life-sharing does not enhance the work? And there is no need for both of them to be standing on the same platform in close proximity because life itself has no requirement that outer forms be beside one another to express in unison.

"So whatever the work, whatever the individual expression in identical at-one-ness, life-sharing, it carries the note of life itself. The door opens. The energies flow through into whatever work we may find we are participating within and at whatever distance or wherever on the planet.

"As group workers become more clearly aware of their inseparable subjective unity this realisation will be more readily understood and expressed."

CHAPTER NINE
Understanding Patterns

Underlying the outer structure of our world are great inner thought patterns through which the evolutionary experiment upon our planet moves into expression. It is humanity's role to work progressively with ideas and concepts and through time to build ever more truly to this great inner blueprint.

In our day we have entered into a time when group work and activity is in the forefront of developing the new ideas and concepts to lead into a new age of opportunity and growth. It will therefore be seen just how important it is that the groups become integrated entities in order to present a unified statement or presentation of their particular aspect or distinguishing contribution. It must be true to that which is in emergence with the evolutionary movement of the time and backed by the inner thought patterns.

Although the quality and capacity of each group member will enrich and enliven the total group expression there can be no focus upon individual personalities with the attendant danger of stimulating the personal aspect. In other words, all must relate to one another as souls and not as the personal, outwardly expressing human being. Well may the individual members of a group express within some individual and destined form of service in their daily lives but their group activity will be other than this. It will see the group integrated as a single entity in a united service. The group identity will be the ruling thought in the group consciousness.

When this stage is achieved then the group is able to work as one in the bringing through of the new thought and its useful formulation within their particular sphere of service.

This activity is greatly enhanced as the group develops the capacity to work consciously from the inner planes of awareness and expression. When intuition guides and minds are free from any sense of separativeness then there is unimpeded contact with the world of reality and inner truth.

Our understanding of the nature of *patterns* is a very useful tool. How often we may look back down the years of an incarnation and see a pattern emerging, which may not have been available to our perception when we were immersed in the living of it.

If we are conscious workers we may observe the unfolding of a life pattern, one in which we have addressed the work we incarnated to do. We may see the many contacts we have made. We note those who touched and moved on to other work and who may be destined to take up a co-working role either in ensuing years or in another lifetime. We see the path we have trodden, choices made, other possibilities that may have been developed, what we may have considered as mistakes but all combining in an ongoing movement within the work of our time.

In the ability to observe and to read life patterns lies the capacity to make the most of experience. Reaction is recognised as wastage of energy, which could more usefully be used in creating anew in line with present understanding and opportunity within the group work.

Also when we understand that our evolution upon this planet is governed by choices often and inevitably made between apparently opposing forces or ideas, then it is realised that if one choice proves to be unwise, to hinder progress, another can be made, another path taken. We need to leave behind 'unworkable experiments', and not hold them to ourselves, as increasingly we build according to spiritual values. There is nothing to be gained by raking through karma. Karma dies a natural death as we proceed upon the upward way. *Onward, upward and through.*

We may also consider *patterns* as they are seen emerging in the scheme of things. As we work from the inner focus, as we direct our lives from that point, we notice that we can say, "Things fall into place." Or they create a pattern that best serves at any time to implement that which is in emergence and just which workers need to be together as part of that piece of work. It is seemingly as though there is an invisible hand at work.

We may venture to say that we are working within the principles of the New Day when we understand this method of operation. We are not working with oppositions, with battles; it is a matter of understanding the flow. This is the Life aspect, the natural flow of life. It may be seen how these thoughts on *patterns* fit within the discoveries concerning *through* and the realisation of identity within a unified or single state of being. The flow of energies moves without obstruction.

Within that area of natural movement we may see the patterns emerging, set off by the intent of the moment and what we are focusing, what we are flowing with. No doubt a magnetic attraction is involved here too because all that will support our intention seems to come together in a moment in time: the right gathering of the right people and the required resources at the right moment – availability without seeming organisation – as against the method of commencing at the opposite end of organisation first and foremost.

We may look back at any time and see patterns as they emerge through our lives. We may also see times of stress or difficulty when things were not flowing. But it is when we see that things were guided by Life itself, by standing within that area of focus, things seem to work out magically. This does not imply we will be relieved of hard work and commitment and the necessity to work for the resolution of world problems.

At moments of great crisis upon the planet we find the forces of change powerfully at work. The effect upon human consciousness serves to force us out of the habitual compliance with a way of seeing and expressing life that may have protected us within certain boundaries, within a well established pattern, while at the same time preventing our movement into a newer, freer, more inclusive vision of greater human unity and interdependence.

Such a moment of extreme crisis has been experienced upon the planet in the year of 2001. As a result we have observed the effects moving ever outward, encompassing the whole world and the awareness of the nations and their people. Dramatic changes are occurring, not only in outer affairs but also in human consciousness and the definition of how we relate to one another, person to person, nation to nation. The outlines of new patterns can be seen emerging affecting all areas of human expression through politics to economics to diplomacy and beyond, reaching into the very core of our living and into our everyday lives. No one is untouched and the vision of the one world and the one humanity hovers on the border of awareness awaiting human recognition and expression.

At such a critical time it is imperative that all true servers of humanity assess their own life patterns and assure that they are in accord with that which life is now making possible, in fact is demanding.

At this point of writing a timely phone call from a co-worker in another country picked up on this theme as he spoke of an experience in his group as follows:

"Every individual must not only stand in their own truth but their speech and actions have to be a true reflection of that inner knowing. When the inner and the outer are synchronous then you cannot engage in any life relationship in the old way because the dynamic shifts, the pattern breaks and transforms the outer circumstance in accordance with the greater truth.

"As the individual engages in this new way not only is the individual pattern broken but a group pattern is forced to change. If an individual stands steadfastly in their truth then they can no longer be shifted into a line of least resistance. This forces the group pattern to change as well."

A group member comments

"How often are the opinions on which we base our daily life decisions really considered, thought through and tested against that inner 'knowing', the intuitive sense? True, most of us read the newspapers (or whatever preferred media) with a somewhat cynical eye – but we may still accept the proffered views as an interim opinion until we learn otherwise or until we 'get around to' thinking about it for ourselves.

"Similarly we might believe views put forward by friends and colleagues who appear to have thought the matter through and so present a pre-prepared logic. But we may never quite get around to testing or disproving their logical pathways against our own life observation and frame of reference. Thus trust and judgement may appear to be in conflict when we view life only from the outside and in terms of habitual personal loyalties.

"Such a carry-over from the Age of Authority subtly steers our thinking and life response away from our responsibility (as divine agents in the world) to view the moment's opportunities unencumbered by the distortions of a view that we have grown beyond. The pattern of a presented logic can seduce us into its acceptance without questioning our true compatibility with it.

"How often when we have delayed too long to register something that has been subtly pressing for consideration, but is eclipsed by the parade of external events, do we later think to ourselves: 'I knew something wasn't right with that' or 'I knew I should have checked up on this' and so on. What is it we *knew*? What is the source and process of this *knowing*? What frame of reference has its anchoring point within us – so deep and sure that it seems it requires a crisis to draw it forth?

"If this knowing is the true gauge of reality, why do we continue to succumb to the incomplete and superficial 'take-away' rationales dispensed by those who, on investigation, may be right but may equally be beguiled by an exclusive selection of details designed to serve a separate and personal motive? When opinions are offered in a definitive self-referencing logic why do we lazily allow our minds to become passive prisoners of those thought-patterns? Of such stuff is prejudice made.

"Thus do lawyers prepare the presentation of evidence in court in order to steer the mental associations along their intended direction. There is a power in formulation, in woven pattern, and we can become cut off from reality by a clever turn of phrase or an authoritative dissertation if we don't check the source and the implied assumptions behind the logic.

"In fact our true guide is our own inner being which is that true essence that is part of, and therefore in touch with, the essence of all things and the cause of those formulations that are true to reality."

* * * * *

We may understand the opportunity and the challenge we all face at this critical moment in time and just how imperative it is that we respond to and from the inner sense of awareness, recognising the soul in all and no longer assessing or reacting in the old, separative terms of reference. The progress of the planet depends on it as we proceed with the unavoidable task of building a greater and more harmonious world pattern, working towards an understanding of a new synthesis of all peoples.

* * * * *

An Essay on Patterns by a co-worker

As anyone realises who travels by train, bus or plane; attends meetings, appointments or interviews; produces crops or other primary goods; works in shifts or business hours; responds to traffic lights and obeys road rules, regulations and laws; our world operates by schedules and seasons. The natural world is ordered by the cyclic rhythms of life breathing into matter in its ordered sequence, injecting more and more of its inspiration into the constantly diversifying and adapting forms.

Life flows, but it does so according to design within the universal dance of spirit and matter as they move together into that marriage which is the expression of the underlying synthesis of all that is. This underlying pattern permeates through all scales and dimensions

– even the atom coheres through its own innate dance. So the great design is reflected through every particle individually and in its co-ordination within larger and larger wholes. And in fact every dimension of our life operates according to pattern – individually and in co-ordination with larger and larger wholes.

Humankind is the conscious reflection of this divine dance. From our primitive beginnings rhythm and music have been the abstract expression of our sense of the patterns of life. They have guided the emotional life through ordered patterns to motivate, celebrate or cohere individuals into common relationship. Our mental life has followed patterns of thought expressed as ideas, ideals and ideologies. And as nature is constantly diversifying and expanding the divine expression, so does the life flow demand constant movement and constant emergence of an increasingly divine manifestation.

However, pattern can become imprisoning where we are consumed by the status quo, by current known life expressions, and where we cease envisioning the next, improved patterns to emerge from the divine inspiration. A computer programmer in determining how to fix a 'bug' in a program must identify the pattern of errors that leads him to the missing or conflicting elements in the program's logic. In the meantime the users of the program work out ways around the problem – a new pattern of use – until it is fixed. Despite the bug, creative activity continues but it becomes centralised around the error and can continue that way for some time.

This is the pattern of an external view and gives us such expressions as "Well, life isn't perfect", "We're only human" and all the other trite admissions of a defeat that will only happen if we acquiesce in it. They are excuses, not reasons, for lack of vision and purpose. They proclaim loudly that we have looked only to the external world for inspiration instead of to the source it obscures.

We are confronted by this circumscribed mediocrity in our daily lives and then see it reflected in the policies of our governments until a shock event shakes the system and enables true leaders to emerge with vision. Tony Blair's speech to the Labour Party conference following the catastrophic events in New York and Washington during September 2001, recognises the opportunity and identifies many of the essentials for new vision:

"There is a coming together. The power of community asserting itself. We are realising how fragile are our frontiers in the face of the world's new challenges. Today conflicts rarely stay within national boundaries. Today a tremor in one financial market is repeated in the markets of the world. Today confidence is global; either its presence or its absence. Today the threat is chaos; because for people with work to do, family life to balance, mortgages to pay, careers to further, pensions to provide, the yearning is for order and stability and if it doesn't exist elsewhere, it is unlikely to exist here. . . . We can't do it all . . But the power of the international community could, together, if it chose to. . . . The kaleidoscope has been shaken. The pieces are in flux. Soon they will settle again. Before they do, let us re-order this world around us. Today humankind has the science and technology to destroy itself or to provide prosperity to all. Yet science can't make the choice for us. Only the moral power of a world acting as a community, can."

Patterns perpetuate by their own dynamic if we do not recognise them and direct them according to life's purpose. They can become destructive of that purpose when allowed to run their own course. One of the most obvious and also most subtle aspects of the legacy of the Piscean patterns of the past is a sense of exclusivity. With the growth of the intellectual power of the race this sense of exclusivity may be rationalised as merely 'difference' but there can also be an underlying sense of 'better', 'more deserving', 'more valuable' than others.

The familiarity of the patterns of thought and feeling (which often sustain us in our times of weakness) can distract from the hidden prejudices and separative motive and then a plethora of rationalisation rises to their continued support. Whenever a single model or pattern is the basis for comprehensive application, it must be questioned if it does not answer for all within its area of application. Whenever current solutions are not working this reactive dynamic is at work.

True vision and solution can flow only from the central blueprint of life itself.

We are told that 'simplification proceeds rapidly as we near the goal of spirit' – but that simplification is from the perspective of spirit not from the perspective of 'rationalising' or 'regimenting' the external detail of our living expression. *What are we?* and *what are we expressing?* are the first questions rather than *how are we expressing?* Self or soul expression will make obsolete the exclusive expression of the little self. The human soul is then in a position to truly reflect the divine human spirit into the world.

In a more worldly rendering of the more immediate realisation Tony Blair states: "The critics will say: but how can the world be a community? Nations act in their own self-interest. Of course they do. But what is the lesson of the financial markets, climate change, international terrorism, nuclear proliferation or world trade? It is that our self-interest and our mutual interests are today inextricably woven together."

Every aspect of our living universe is ordered by pattern and rhythm. Music, mathematics, geometry, art, architecture, the investigative and social sciences, philosophies and theologies are all patterns of disciplined activity as we identify and make manifest the essential patterns of life. But where is the source of the inspiration that breathes life into them, through them? Are we merely reacting to form life and so creating 'more of the same', going in circles, or are we responding to new waves of inspiration, creating new forms that are expansive enough to house our growing realisation of that life more abundant that flows through all from the point where spirit and matter are one?

Life and movement are synonymous and the moment we cast our lot with the status quo we have opted for death. Life brings destruction to old forms as new ones are birthed but death clings to forms, separateness and exclusivity. Ultimately all is enlivened by the living power of the universe no matter how temporal. When life directs the patterns through time and space we have a divine Plan.

Chapter ten
Sensitivity

The growth or development of sensitivity is behind the evolutionary process. It is not about being endowed with senses or a responsive sense apparatus and sent forth into the world but in conjunction with the evolutionary forces and our environment, senses develop. Sensitivity implies a ready or an acute response to some stimulus or other. It is basic to our ability to apprehend and to know anything. And this depends on the capacity or the refinement of our vehicles of expression at any moment in time to respond with accuracy and understanding to whatever is in any dimension of the environment – physical, emotional, mental or spiritual.

That which *is* – the revelation we may seek – is everywhere present and at every moment. It is only the lack of sensitivity of the vehicles of expression we are using at any moment that hides it from us, whether in part or some essence of it or in its entirety. With this thought in mind we may see sensitivity as the capacity to apprehend the subtle dimension, that which is emerging.

We are challenged to develop a truly sensitive apparatus and to use it to stretch our capacity to imagine, to incorporate, to see that whatever it is we are approaching always has a higher counterpart, to see ever greater wholes. In this process we increase the ability to anticipate that which is next or that which hovers just beyond the borders of our present awareness. So do we develop a more subtle sense but only as we acknowledge the possibility and move in sensitive awareness into another area of contact and response.

Unless we embrace the understanding that evolution or expansion of consciousness – progress through time and space, through eternity, through the universe – is never static, then we will come to a point where we will just atrophy. This is the mistake that has been made by any orthodox school of thought throughout time, often by placing one great leader or another in a position of perfection, as being the 'only begotten', the only 'spokesperson' of Deity. The teacher becomes deified and the followers never understand that he is demonstrating what we all must become.

Through the evolutionary process, through this increasing realisation of perfecting in one system after another, we find the story of sensitivity. During the past age our teachers in the field of religion have shut the door to expansion of awareness to a great extent. In other fields, such as science, the door is ajar because science recognises that it never has the final statement and is open to further discovery. Religion desperately needs to move onward and, as we are told, into the Life aspect. Actually, it is life that is missing.

We may understand that we cannot move on into these increasing areas of sensitivity that bring us an awareness of ever greater, deeper, wider states of realisation unless we can conceive of the possibility – unless we can develop the capacity to imagine, to visualise what may lie ahead, not necessarily in detail but a realisation of its magnitude, and not as an impossible goal – as something we attain to. Thus we develop a preparatory sensitivity to that which lies ahead, a sensitivity that will relate us to, identify us with, enable us to recognise these higher states as we approach them. The door is open.

We find ourselves returning to that thought of going through the curtain of our own human nature, and perhaps of our own soul nature. *Through.* Until we discover where we are going. We are however already contained within that life. We use words like 'going' because the whole idea is related to life; it is related to movement. There is no point where anything is stationary and therefore in a state of breaking down. That is death. Static conditions mean death. The withdrawal of life is death. And, my friends, there is no death. There is only life in all dimensions.

So as we develop this sensitivity, this preparatory sensitivity, we move increasingly into ever-greater areas of recognition of life itself. And just as it is said that we tread the path and eventually realise we are the path itself, it is spun out of our very own being, then we come to the stage where we *know* that our being is one with Being itself, a state of being which we share along with every other entity as conscious parts within one whole.

Through every dimension sensitivity is our guide and teacher whether it be within the average human field of living, within intuitive levels of spiritual sensitivity or within higher levels of sensitive response to divine purpose. And if we care to look towards even more exalted expressions of Life we will find that the great sun Sirius has been called the 'Brilliant Star of Sensitivity'.

Traps for Young Players

As we think about developing or increasing sensitivity in order to better serve the work of our time it is useful to recognise traps we may fall into. These may be difficult to recognise as we find ourselves immersed in the learning process. We may even be unaware that they can, in fact, exist.

Once again, the problem and the challenge lies in the fact that we have such a facility in identifying with the teaching or the methodology which we may elect to use to steer our course, that we can unknowingly become trapped within the process itself. There are many useful methods and printed works that can provide us with very sound instruction and pointers to the Way. However, we must never lose sight of the fact that this is all they are and they are in themselves not that which we seek.

How often we may take a course or read a book and our focus of attention is normally and naturally upon the material itself. Our intention may well be the discovery of what these sources can reveal but we have to realise that which we seek is other than the means and, in fact, does not resemble it. Can we see energy? Can we see experience per se? Let us distinguish between learning and its process, and experience. And let us understand the value and the use of the subtle sensitivity awaiting our recognition.

If, when we have read any profound teaching, we are asked whether we really understand it, do we believe we are being asked whether we have the capacity to extend our understanding to absorb yet another layer of the truth? Perhaps this may be so. But more significantly we are being shown that the word description of the mechanisms and the forces that drive the universe and the worlds we live in, cannot bring us to realisation. It is only when that centre, that source of *knowing*, is touched and awakened within us that the emerging reality of Life and its living processes dawns upon our consciousness, is released into our awareness and expression.

Any written or spoken exposition of the deeper truths may give us much useful information but it is another thing altogether to find the release of our knowing whereby we become conscious directors of these energies and participating expressions of Life itself.

As a group we have focused our thought upon that word *through* and have endeavoured to find its *releasing power*. Initially we have set about defining its movement and the mechanism of its operation. Our minds do this and automatically swing in to aid the exercise. Minds are developed tools. But where is that subtle sensitivity that alone may apprehend the subtle worlds of our true being and deliver into our hands the ability to move in conscious awareness through the unfolding dimensions of life opening out before us?

So we have used that word *through* to move, to free up energy, within our life expression or within the work we do but there are many, many other 'forms' or 'devices' we may choose to employ for the purpose. We must always remember that the form is representative only of that which we seek and behind every form is life or energy.

Don't be trapped!

As had happened before, while writing this chapter a caller made contact and spoke about a workshop that she and a close co-worker had just presented. During a role-play discussion around inclusive community building the group became aware that although they were all well intentioned about inclusiveness, the languaging and therefore the dynamic in the moment polarised around 'we' and 'the others'. A shift occurred as everyone suddenly realised how they were thinking and speaking about their intention. In that moment there was a breakthrough and they realised they had a common goal.

Sensitive to their common intention, together they passed through the apparent outer differences of view into a true realisation and demonstration of the nature of inclusiveness. They changed the dynamic by changing their approach from outer and separated emphases to that inner sensitivity which revealed the reality of that which they were addressing: inclusiveness.

CHAPTER ELEVEN
Once upon a Time

In a transitional moment in time such as we now experience, as we leave behind the evening of the sign Pisces with its peculiar energies and enter the morning of Aquarius we are confronted by a confusion of energies and ideas, both old and new. Those people who work within the Piscean energies may firmly believe they are implementing the Aquarian thinking for the time but if we observe the operation we will note that these workers are often engaged in protecting or promoting a point of view which, although it has had its day of usefulness, is what they have always embraced and they cannot comfortably accept change nor recognise the new necessity.

The exponents of the new day in Aquarius see (to varying degrees of clarity) the changes that are needed and why. But they face a different challenge than the former group of workers. They are not in the position of any necessity to protect a system because obviously it has not yet been established. We see them working, therefore, in an entirely different way and with different energies. Herein lies the challenge of a transitional time.

The following stories address some of the difficulties encountered by group workers as the rather different energies appear to come into conflict when workers come together to cooperate in some form of service. We observe the polarised positions of thinking and of expression as they are placed side by side. It is only as all are able to work from the point of inner oneness that such difficulties may be resolved.

* * * * *

The Sacred Space

Once upon a time in a very beautiful land two companions stood upon the side of a high hill looking out upon the beauties of the natural world. One said, "This is a sacred space and we must protect it for our Lord." The Other replied, "We are sacred people and we thus imbue this space." The One said, "We must be silent and not allow disruption of the quiet countryside." The Other replied, "If we know silence within there will be silence without." Then the wind sprang up and played through the trees and rustled their leaves. And the One said, "Hush." And the Other said, "The wind sings the song of our Lord." A flock of crows flew over calling, "caw caw, caw caw." The One said, "Hush you birds. You make such a disturbance in this sacred space." And the crows replied, "Caw caw, caw caw."

Then a group of children came tumbling down the hill, all shouting and laughing with delight, their dog leaping in their midst with joyous barks. The One said, "Children be quiet, be still. It is not seemly to act so rowdily in this sacred space." The Other said, "The children sound the note of innocence of the natural world. They belong to this realm." A troubadour followed after the children playing his stringed instrument in accompaniment with their joy. And they danced along with him. The One said, "Silence, silence!" And the Other sang a joyful verse.

They became aware of a Presence standing with them and He spoke of the Coming Time that already was upon them and the understanding of Oneness that was flowering, freeing his people from the restrictions that had sprung up in the past and that had denied the true, free expression of spirit – their natural birthright that flows without the rules and regulations made by human thoughts. The wind carried his words across the countryside and onward to circle the globe, gathering in volume and awakening the minds of all who heard. The people were drawn to the Voice of the Teacher and they sat in great numbers upon the hillside and once again listened to the words of their Master. And they said, "This is indeed a sacred space and it dwells within us. We must go forth and tell the whole world." The children replied, "Do you not remember? He told us this before – a long time ago. But now we must know how to *live* it."

So the children led the way and they all moved down the hillside and out into the township and to the cities and into the whole world. The people awakened from the deep sleep of enchantment, from the spell woven by the world of forms. And the sacred space was to be found everywhere and in everyone across the whole world. How could it ever be otherwise?

And they all *lived* ever after…

* * * * *

The One and the Other

Down in the township two teachers met to consider the needs of the children in their charge. They were wise and they understood that the children needed guidance on their pathway through life, alongside the basic training of their minds that would fit them for the world of everyday.

The One said, "We must give them a set of *rules* within which to steer their course. This way is tried and true through many generations."

The Other said, "Our generation is responsible for apprehending and holding the new vision for our world so that we may guide the youth according to the *principles* involved."

The One said, "In all the temptations and problems of today's world the youth need the security of a set of rules."

The Other replied, "Today's young people cannot be confined within prescribed forms. They do not respond to the past ways; their eyes are focused upon the future. They *are* the future."

The One said, "They do not yet have life experience. We must teach them the *precepts* to guide their steps."

The Other responded, "We must teach the young people *life principles* and reveal them through our own life expression."

A small group of young people entered the room, asking if they may speak with the teachers. They told the story of certain needs they had become aware of in their community and within their peer group and asked what could be done to assist.

The One said, "We will attend to this need."

The Other said, "Learn to assist by assisting. You know what is needed. Let that sacred space within you reach and touch the sacred space within those you would help."

The young people went out and gathered their peer group together to talk about the needs and the challenges they all faced. The small group spoke to their friends and companions about the advice of their teachers and the instruction that they should find their way by showing others.

Said one young person, "But how do we help when we don't know how to help ourselves?"

Another added, "Sometimes I know what's needed but it is so hard to find the words to express what I want to say – yet inwardly I know. Does that make sense?"

"Yes," replied one of the small group. "But if you know what's there to be said you need to 'touch' the other person to draw it forth. That's what our teacher told us – to let that inner place in us touch that place in others."

"What do you mean?" asked the boy.

"Well, we have learned about the magnetic forces – we have learned about the Law of Attraction…"

"Yes…"

"If you allow that within you to touch that within another, the energies combining will set in motion – and set free – that thought within you that will flow outward in words to the other person you would help."

"How?"

"We are all spiritual beings, we are souls, and live in a world of Oneness. We are each and all inwardly in touch with one another. When our thought is off ourselves and what we want – or what we can't do – it is no longer dammed up in the small box of the personal self. It no longer exists in a separated state but flows freely between beings."

The small group had responded to the recognition of a need and had taken the responsibility to act. As they spoke with their companions they found that they were in fact demonstrating the principle in action that they had been seeking to explain. The whole group continued to confer – they penetrated deeply into the realisation of Oneness and found that together they were becoming aware of a way of work.

The young people went out and discovered that obvious but hidden truth: they *knew* because they worked and not because they took training to serve. They realised they were working with the living energies moving throughout the whole. They were focused outward in service from the sacred centre of their being and were not merely focused upon themselves. And they knew that Oneness is the only reality.

* * * * *

The Children's Round Table

The following story is based on a dream of a group member.

Within a great castle in the New World the children were gathered in their numbers to demonstrate to their Elders just how they all worked together around the New Round Table. As the Knights of Old, they were governed by a unity of purpose and Truth was their watchword.

Each child knew that they all had their inner teacher, the true Self within, but they were also aware of the Enlightened Ones who advised and instructed them once they had recognised their own inner teacher and had begun to live their lives in response.

On this day one of the children, whose name was John, was to play his role as leader of the group. The Teacher spoke with the children and finally asked, "Are you ready, John?"

"Yes," said John.

"Are you all ready, children?" He asked.

"Yes," they all chorused.

The children filed into the large, central hall where the Elders were assembled and took their places at the Round Table, each placing a magical medallion on the table in front of them. The magical medallions represented each one's own unique gift to the group and would not allow the expression of anything other than Truth. They emitted a discordant sound if perchance anything less than truth was spoken or thought.

John drew out a scroll and began to speak together with the other children about various issues and all added their thought in the ensuing discussion. At intervals they took a vote and each time the children responded with a vibrant 'yes', together and as one pounding their fists on the table. The sound broke the remnants of the old order to smithereens.

The intuition was already alive in these children and their minds clear, uncluttered and intelligent. They knew the mind to be an instrument, a servant of their group purpose; it did not govern. So united were they that they had come to understand and to operate as a 'group leader' and were therefore of great usefulness within the field of the work, inspiring other groups by their very livingness. Whatever the need or focus of the work at any time, one member would move forward as leader according to their quality or special gift but at no time was any one of them aware of expressing other than as the unity which they were as they moved as one out into the world of service and creative expression.

An Elder asked, "Children, what is the source of your unity?"

One replied, "Life itself is the Source of our unity. We are drawn together in response to the divine Plan for our time and together are charged to bring it forth into the light of day. Unity cannot be imposed nor can it be conformed to an outwardly chosen goal. It emerges from the reality known within. Then, and only then, does it flower forth in beauty and in expression for the common good. Unity walks hand in hand with love. The people crave unity but it cannot be enforced any more than can peace."

A second Elder questioned, "Children, have you observed how our records of history show our race making the same errors over and over again? What is the cause of this?"

Another replied, "Throughout time we have learned much but we have failed to learn one basic lesson – that we are spiritual beings. We have approached life and one another as separated personal beings, failing to understand that these forms were being perfected in order to express the spiritual world and our spiritual natures through the world of forms – to bring the spirit into expression through the world of matter. We learn from the past – we build for the future."

Said a third Elder, "Children, speak to us of change."

A third child replied, "Change is unavoidable, inevitable, in the onward movement of evolution. If we work within the spiritual principles we serve with wisdom to implement the change necessary for the progress of our world. People fear change because it appears to threaten the familiar to which they cling in their everyday lives. This again results from a belief in a world governed by separation. It is only that which has served its purpose, that which now begins to crystallise, that is swept aside for the life-giving principle to bring forth the new thought and expression to guide our world on the next stage of its onward journey. In such selfless action true freedom is born."

Once again an Elder questioned, "Children, are you sure you are right? How do you assess what is needed and your action in response?"

Another child stood to reply, "By the use of our divine subtle sense that observes the One Whole. This view encompasses time and place and enables us to position the elements needed within suitable forms and with right timing."

Yet another Elder asked, "How do the new forms differ from those developed for the Age which now withdraws?"

A child's reply was prompt, "In the time fast passing the forms themselves received much focused attention. The soul of all things was not so clearly recognised. The spirit seemed far removed and was not understood as our true being. It therefore attracted fear or devotion and other aspects related to the sense of remoteness. Seekers endeavoured to reach a divinity seen as outside oneself. As this New Age has been dawning it has opened the doors to the realisation of our true identity with the spiritual world and we have begun to create forms of expression in our outer world that reflect the spirit. We are not now so much *reaching inwards* as in the past but are recognising our responsibility as representatives of Soul *to work from within outwards*, to anchor the new ideas and concepts and to build anew. The energies of this time inspire and assist such building."

Commented an Elder, "And yet we see so many, many forms of the old order functioning in all fields of human endeavour."

A child responded, "Change that is sound is not so rapid. But it is being recognised that forms were made to serve and not to be served. Comparisons reveal the obvious in the working of groups. For instance, where there is a dependence or insistence upon forms of procedure to the detriment of the free movement of the work or the workers, curtailing expansion, outreach and speed, and tying the hands of the new workers then it is not long before the honest server will observe what is happening – and what is not – and move into the true understanding of group expression. Unless this is understood a group cannot survive. A searching check into individual motivation is revealing when such group challenges arise."

An Elder asked a final question, "How do you propose to reveal the demands of the New Day?"

John spoke for them all, "By revealing the unity we know and experience, through our words, through our lives and the living expression of our group."

The questions had come to an end and John moved to close the Round Table meeting. All present sounded a great Invocation. The children filed out as they had come.

The Elders gathered in a close circle of review and voiced their consensus: "The children are ready. The future is assured." As one, the Elders withdrew behind the scenes and left the new generation to serve the New World in its New Day.

* * * * *

The Wise One

In the depths of the forest there lived a very wise old man. No one in the towns had ever seen him but they heard tell that there were those in their grandparents' day who at times had caught a glimpse of him through the trees deep, deep in the forest. But still no one knew of anyone living or departed this world who had reported meeting him face to face or speaking with him.

It was said that the Wise One came out among the people when the world passed through the changes of a New Day. And still no one had heard stories of his appearing that could in any way be proven.

There were those who had dreamed of him and he had shown them wondrous things in their sleep. They had wakened to the dawn with a new awareness, and touched by some divine impulse, went forth to work selflessly for the good of their fellows.

And there were those who had ventured deep into the forest never again to return to their community. No search ever found any trace of them. In every generation there were always a small number who disappeared in this way.

At a time when their world was greatly challenged by the forces of darkness a group of the Selfless Ones set out into the forest to search for the Wise One to ask his help, to bring his wisdom to enlighten the people of the towns and to teach them the true meaning of love and compassion.

The townsfolk were a law-abiding people who governed and maintained order by living according to the rules laid down in their society. Departure from the rules was not tolerated and the town Elders had great difficulty to contain the Selfless Ones within such confinement. The Selfless Ones showed more concern for human need than for observation of the rules on how they should do things.

The town Elders were not sorry to see the Selfless Ones depart on their journey into the forest, hoping they would not see them again.

It was not many hours before the Selfless Ones stopped to rest in a space within the forest where the sunlight filtered down through the canopy and sparkled upon the surface of a magical pond. A gentle breeze ruffled the surface of the water and a white mist arose and swirled around and about the Selfless Ones.

A strange and mysterious malaise came over them all and the world began to change around them. Then the breeze sprang up anew and the mist drifted away; the scene became clear once more and before them stood the Wise One together with the many pilgrims who had joined him through the past times.

The Selfless Ones dropped to their knees but the Wise One said, "Stand up, my friends, we have work to do. In a little while we will all go forth into the world to bring the Light to the New Day."

Said one of the Selfless Ones, "How is it so few can find you, oh Wise One? Who may find you?"

The Wise One replied, "Only the pure in heart."

The Gift of the Ages

At a certain point in time and space the two brothers, Pisces and Aquarius, met together to confer regarding the charge given them by the Great Lord to imbue the human kingdom with their energies and enable the people to grow in understanding and wisdom in due course of time.

They spoke together of the gifts that Pisces had bestowed upon this world throughout a long Age and how the humanity had responded and grown and had been infused with the very living energies of Pisces himself. They now portrayed many more characteristics and qualities than they had before the coming of Pisces.

But now Pisces was yielding the Day to his brother, Aquarius, to conduct humanity into yet another day in which humanity would absorb and express anew, retaining all past gain, leaving behind all but the true essence of the passing time and progressing under the energies of Aquarius.

Pisces spoke, "I have watched this humanity grow as I have imbued them with my energies and stirred them to a sensitive response. They are far more attentive to the inner voice than had been possible in the past. They have learned the lesson of self-denial blossoming forth in the understanding of sacrifice, the ability to redeem and to make things holy. They can easily identify with the needs of others but at times they may identify to the degree of losing the sense of self in those they seek to aid. As I hand over to you my brother, Aquarius, I know you will lead my charges upon the next stage of their Way."

Aquarius answered his brother, "My energies will teach this race a loving, more impersonal service to their fellows. I pour myself out as the Water of Life to a world athirst for a new vision to inspire a New Day, a new way of salvation."

Said Pisces, "Salvation during my Day has been hard won. Its mark has been the Cross and all who responded to my energies sought freedom from the prison of the material world. Perceiving their spiritual selves but closed in by the world of matter, they have indeed drunk of the cup of sorrow as they have fought towards freedom, reaching upwards towards the heavens. But I can see, my brother, your energies will reveal the truth that the spirit is invincible, the outer world is what anyone may make it. The people will find strength in this knowledge and know the joy of life."

Aquarius responded, "Without your energies first to imbue, to inspire and to lay the foundation it would not be possible for me to take humanity on a step further in their evolutionary journey. They themselves have arrived at a point at which they can recognise this unfolding process. When this is truly understood the new freedom is gained. That which has served its purpose, has completed its usefulness, is allowed to decline in favour of that which will lead on to greater realisation and expression of greater things. While the true essence of all that has been learned remains in the living character of the people, never to be lost. It is what they presently are, reflections of your energies, my brother, Pisces."

Pisces spoke again, "The true race in Pisces is compassionate, patient and responds inclusively to the needs of others. We may observe the many great servers who have worked tirelessly throughout the centuries to better the lives of their fellow beings. They have indeed set forth to save. And they are already moving with the flow into the new possibilities."

Aquarius replied, "The race in Aquarius will build upon these attributes. They will also display humanitarianism and inclusiveness. Their life demonstration will expand into the expression of universality as they are challenged to recognise the Oneness of all, inclusive of every nation, creed and colour and to value the contribution of every part within the diverse tapestry of human life in expression. And most importantly they will develop *the true group server* as they band together in their groups, drawn by the particular work that they have come to do and by those who are theirs to work with. They will understand the spirit of sharing in all things. They will be forward looking and innovative as they work with the new energies in service for the benefit of all."

Said Pisces, "You will note that during the Age wherein I have breathed forth my energies humanity has given birth to the great creative poets, composers and painters. The arts have flourished and the imagination has burst forth within the race preparing the way for the growth of the intuition within the field of your energies, my brother Aquarius."

Added Aquarius, "And the intuition will open the door to vaster dimensions of experience and of living, and human consciousness will express a new creativity and understand love in its higher sense. The future is upon our doorstep and all must step through."

Observed Pisces, "We are both aware that humanity can so easily interpret and express our energies in a negative way. That happens when anyone feels separate from others and has forgotten the unity and interdependence within which all live and have their being. However, it is in the nature of growth in consciousness on this planet Earth that its humanity must have the opportunity of choice, of experiment and of experience. This is part of the divine Plan."

Aquarius spoke to the future, "Such is the increasing clarity of vision of the people of this time that they are intensely aware of the results of past choices that have brought them to this point. They see their world as it now appears and they know that they are its creators. They face many challenges and opportunities and many situations that must be resolved and turned to good account. There is also much of goodness, of beauty and of truth that they have brought into their world. They have grown in spirit. With their response to my Aquarian energies and their group-conscious spirit they will build anew according to the Plan of the Great Lord and so will usher in the New Day."

Pisces took leave of his brother Aquarius and withdrew slowly into his place while Aquarius waxed in strength, joyfully pouring out the Water of Life upon the Earth and upon her peoples.

*****

Remember: the One ever contains all others.

CHAPTER TWELVE
Anecdotes along the Road

As I have been writing this book I have been vividly aware all the time of the pressure from the inner planes and the presence of inner friends. It seems I hardly have to think it out and yet it is a matter of a continual, unwavering point of tension and continuous work. Thus focused, it has been a matter of 'downloading' the flow from the inner levels of awareness and of living.

Looking back through the work of this lifetime I can observe how the inner planes have always guided me along the Way and often with apparently strange methods. It has been a matter of seizing upon many and varied impressions that seemed to be attracting my attention, telling me something, directing my thought to observe, interpret or decipher.

This has urged me to investigate all possibilities – to crawl under, over, around and through whatever came into my range of contact. It prompted one co-worker to make the comment, "It is a matter of seeing something in everything even when there is nothing (no thing) there!" In fact, there is nothing in this world that does not have a lesson of some kind to teach us or the capacity to reveal life's hidden recesses to our view. But that which is impressed directly upon our awareness from our inner Source is far more specific and related to our particular area or function in the world work. Whatever we contact and make ours we *must* use in service.

Very early in this life's work, like many another server, there was a great impulse to search out a clear and directive picture of the way ahead. What details may be seen in such a picture? What choices could or should be made? Could I be correct in assessment in the midst of uncertainty? Many other searching questions tumbled through my mind. And then I found myself swept into an unusual waking experience.

It seemed that I was moving upwards through planes, passing then through a space I could only call at the time 'no man's land' and onward until I looked down upon the scene below me. I observed a long straight dirt road and I stood half way along that road. The picture immediately conveyed to my mind the message it held.

Before entering into incarnation the path is already set, laid out before us. We have only to walk it. In fact, we already *know* it. It is not seen as the polarity between beginning and end – it is a completed whole. The questions I had been asking were questions about the details of the life and its work and the understanding needed to fulfil these requirements. However, the important thing to recognise is that we may express only what we *are* at any moment in time. The details – how and what we express as we meet the circumstances and opportunities of life – are worked out in those moments and directed by that which we have brought with us in terms of understanding and awareness of the spiritual principles.

There can be no turning back. There is only the path straight ahead. The only errors we can make are: attempting to turn back; stopping in one place; departure from the path or turning aside from the task; and failing to advance wholeheartedly using *everything* we are and have for the sake of the work of the time.

About this time, in the early-to-mid sixties, 'new' thoughts were appearing to my focused attention. Deep pondering opened the door upon some vision or another which increasingly revealed more and more the nature and function of the inner worlds that informed and drove the outer world. Although I was working with groups, the truly esoteric group had not yet begun to gather and I felt very much on my own (a great illusion!) in my search.

One day while closely examining some issue or another I became aware of an aggravatingly large patch of blotches in front of my sight. Suddenly I had the sensation of movement backwards at considerable speed. The blotchy dots receded and from a distance now were seen to form the pixels comprising a face that regarded me. I understood the necessity to stand back and take the total view – see the whole – work from the universal to the particular.

But it was not finished. Next I found myself standing in inner awareness at a bay's edge. Trees lining the shores were reflected in the water and a gentle rippling of the surface of the water presented a distorted but fascinating image. Again I was moving at speed coming to a stop at the top of a high cliff looking down upon the same body of water. What a greatly changed picture revealed itself! The scene startled me. Reflected in the mirror below me was the image of the Divine Life. To attempt to define it further is impossible.

How important to stand back – not to be caught myopically in the foreground of life, the little personal world with its claims to primary reality and its oft-times enchanting scene! And more importantly, to recognise the far vaster spiritual reality which substands all outer seeming – to work from the world of cause and not be confused and deceived by the world of effects. Only then may we build according to the true spirit of our time.

Even film captured my attention and made revelation. Watching the film *Joan of Arc* one finds this heroine portrayed as a martyr and indeed such she was. But viewed symbolically and observing the story as an analogy of the life of every disciple, one may note that every true world server can never identify with the idea of 'the martyr'. The true worker demands the utmost of all vehicles, physical, emotional and mental – the whole three-fold personality – and never acts to save or protect these personal forms from the rigours of the work and its fiery nature.

The response is ever to the demands of the soul and the needs of the work. It is a response made under the Law of Sacrifice. Again this is not seen as 'giving up' something, as does the martyr, but rather of 'taking over' responsibility to work on behalf of the human race with very much of the work proceeding behind the scenes, unknown and unrecognised by any other than those who work together consciously in the subtle dimensions of life. The disciple's identity is merged with that of the inner group of workers and together they work according to the divine plan.

Another film with a comment on today's work and workers is *Imitation General*. The General is by no means the usual general. He did not remain in secure position way behind the lines but joined his troops up front in the thick of the action. He was an inspiration to the men who felt they could achieve anything required under his leadership.

During the action told within the film the General and his troop found themselves trapped within a wood surrounded by the enemy. As they awaited the arrival of reinforcements the General devised many clever ways to confuse the enemy and deceive them into the belief that there were a considerably greater number of troops within the wood. As a result of enemy fire the General was killed. A soldier with the rank of private discovered the General's body and hid it in a shed in the wood, knowing that the morale of the men would suffer if they realised the General had died.

The soldier took the General's helmet – his five-pointed star – upon him and proceeded to direct operations with similar ability. The troops held out until the arrival of the reinforcements at which time the soldier, having suffered a blow to the head was lying unconscious. The new arrivals discovered the General's body in the shed and presumed he had just been killed in the final assault of the enemy prior to their arrival. Since the soldier was unconscious he received neither commendation nor a court martial for impersonating an officer.

When the day is done the soldier blends back into the ranks, unknown and unsung by the external world, but possessed of the realisation of a task well done, and a deepened understanding of that great Law of Sacrifice and the capacity to save.

Here is the modern day disciple, taking the 'five-pointed star' upon the self, acting within the Work as one who has assumed the responsibility and the realisation of the Soul – an inspiration and a rallying point for the work and for the workers. This disciple leads as one with the whole group and by the living demonstration of selfless and intuitive service. No safe retreat here. This disciple is in the thick of it, and demanding the utmost from self, draws those souls who are co-workers in service together and as a group.

Life continued to play the teacher and much was learned about the Aquarian principle of service and its methods. The esoteric group began to gather. It became clear that in one sense it was so much easier to work alone. The difficulties presented by early group work wherein personalities frequently could disrupt and delay the work, was not a factor. However, since we had entered the Age of Aquarius with its group awareness and expression it was essential, indeed unavoidable, that the work must proceed in group formation. It was subsequently realised that so very much more was open to discovery when working within a group containing as it did such a valuable collection of souls, minds and hearts of varying outreach, expression and qualities.

By the end of 1969 the Group was in full operation and the 'instruction' continued as before but now in terms of the Group and its work as a whole. Esoteric advice was received by group members but only in terms of effects on or within the Group, its life and work.

At this time a 'message' was received by impression for each group member which spoke clearly to the individual while holding within it deeper insights that could progressively be recognised and implemented in service. As the individual penetrated into the inner worlds that which was 'hidden' could be accessed in an ongoing way, revealing deeper meaning and significance throughout a lifetime. It was as if these words were recorded on cassette tape and could be played through at will within one's attentive awareness.

As time went by other methods and processes of group impression emerged. One such entailed the following: During a group meeting it was suggested on impulse that all members write on a slip of paper a word or phrase that would define the opposite of the verb 'to give'. Of the eight people present at this meeting there was no duplication of answer. This seemed surprising. The slips of paper were collected together and dropped into the back of a notebook without further thought.

Nine months later (gestation period) there was the impression to retrieve these answers and 'match' each one beside the consciousness of the respective individuals. It was quite a revelation and considerably useful to each member concerned. Each one had spoken from their own awareness and the outpicturing or unfolding understanding was clearly to be seen in process of emergence demonstrating just where the member stood, both individually and within the group work, and directing their course ahead.

A few examples of the choices made in response to the question "What is the opposite of the verb 'to give'?" plus their assessment nine months later follow below. They have been taken from the journal record of December 1972.

> Pr: 'To receive' – thought process: first thought "the usually recognised opposite word of 'to give' is 'to take'." This brings reaction in the individual to that condition in humanity of taking, grasping, selfishness. Second thought "it is more blessed to give than to receive." Answer decided on, therefore, 'to receive' because even though it is more blessed to give, it must to some degree be blessed to receive and this is much preferable to 'taking'. There was no deeply considered thought beyond these steps or stage. Pr has a great capacity to reach a vast majority of people in today's world who are swinging to this understanding.
>
> Ne: 'Hold' – a recognition that it is a mistake to give to 'children' anything that cannot yet be handled, for which they are not yet ready. Drawn first into teaching of children in the actual sense – symbolic of the work of teaching those young in spirit. Ne has a great sympathetic rapport with these people (on both sides

of the veil). Works well on the astral plane where for safety, emotion must be kept in balance. Through service will learn to fill the needs (learning-wise) of these people. The word 'hold' may also be understood as 'not rushing in' – the mind must be brought in here as the determining factor, or instrument of decision – always. In other words, well considered action.

As with Pr, Ne will fill a vital position as distributor (in group work and out from the group) – a great responsibility not to be underestimated in its importance and value at this particular moment (thereby lessening its effectiveness) for it is preparing the way or setting a pattern for further building or development which will follow in the work of others involved in the 'next' or another phase (not of 'time' but of expression).

There is no recognition as yet of the fuller significance 'withhold'. 'Hold' implies 'to keep in trust' while the way is prepared for greater or broader recognition, while 'withhold' suggests that one who has this ability has come into a knowledge of the truth which is revealed (to others) only by his or her radiation and understood or received by any 'recipient' to the degree of their own capacity. It allows or permits stimulation only at soul levels.

C-c: 'Relinquish' – reveals a need to fix the eyes upon the object of service or that which is being served rather than upon any thought of 'preparing the server to serve'. The soul is very wise and knows exactly what occult service means and is abundantly capable. The esoteric service stage has definitely been reached. Throw off forever all conventional thought – *this* relinquish – for it will condition and restrict your service. An aura of conventional attitude persists. It is not by any means overpowering but appears as a faint haze and can easily be unnoticed or overlooked by the individual. Because it is so nebulous it can constitute a danger to unimpeded soul expression and it must be disintegrated with a deliberate and final forcefulness.

Ar: 'Withold' – not yet a complete recognition but close. The omission of a letter from the word was known as a possibility at the time of writing. It holds no great importance, as personalities think, in regard to correct spelling but nevertheless occultly reveals incompletion of a particular recognition rather than error (which would be occultly represented by a wrongly chosen letter symbol – omission is another matter). There is a significant vibration surrounding the thought in this particular response. It lies in the fact, or is defined by Ar's recognition that the word 'may have a letter missing' – that the state of incompletion does not exist because Ar has not yet recognised the step to completion or fullness (as contained in the definition of 'withhold' at the end of Ne's notes) but that she 'sees', if not with absolute certainty, that which is omitted, that which will bring forth or allow of soul service unrestrained and unrestricted.

La: 'Retain' – That which is retained in this case is the same as that which is withheld. But the situation is different. *That* is seen and known but the channel of outgoing is not wide open. (Surprised?) Where wisdom dictates that a flood of brilliance be occultly 'withheld' (conscious soul work) that one may serve by stimulation by degree, 'to retain' suggests that our *knowing* is not completely available to all and sundry according as they would demand (esoterically or unconsciously). This does not suggest personal selfishness for at this point that is not a factor but rather a misapplication of the meaning of the term 'isolated unity' – perhaps indicating a first ray focus. The world task and the need are fully recognised, the *knowing* or wisdom is not in question – response must be drawn into objectivity without restraint or restriction.

These were still early days of the Group and learning processes ever continued to change, to expand and to become more deeply esoteric in nature. As time went by the individual was no longer addressed as such but was merged within the group life. 'Instruction' or impression then became a concentrated focus upon the group work.

For some time individuals became aware of, or interpreted, the ideas contacted in symbolic form and at our meetings invariably found a dovetailing of each one's discoveries with those of the other members. A larger picture of what was emerging was then seen incorporating each person's viewpoint, quality or type and how it could be used in service. Eventually impression became more direct and we called this stage 'the Group coming out from behind its symbols'.

Towards the end of 1984 a Group member joined with representatives of various schools of thought at an inner plane meeting to discuss causes of world problems and to ponder thoughts of resolution. There appeared some difficulty in communication due to the variety of emphases, points of importance and the general background of the participants. It was a moment to leave behind formal presentation and speak from the heart. One person was recorded speaking as follows:

"Our world is seemingly divided by nations and their cultures, races and ideologies. When people come together to discuss resolution of world problems we find that even such dedicated and concerned people can be further divided by semantics and by their background and the forms through which they express.

"We need to get to the *heart* of the problem. We need to speak *from the heart*. The human mind has seen such tremendous growth; it can outweigh the heart, seemingly. The heart and mind need to be a balanced team. Human capacity to make discovery in the areas of science, technology and so on, the mental and analytical ability, has expanded enormously – especially noted since the demands made upon scientific expertise by World War II. There is no suggestion that we should deny the fruits of such progress – this phase in human history has developed to the full the analytical, critical mind. We see 'the parts' in everything and this can temporarily obscure the fact of the basic unity, the underlying synthesis, of all life. Human unity is indeed a fact.

"When some of us were speakers at an interstate conference midyear we were asked to leave our 'satchels of ideas' at home – not to emphasise our own particular approaches but to communicate together with the recognition of our basic human unity. The conference theme was 'The Healing of the Nations – a personal purpose'.

"We have all assembled here with the one purpose. We are all concerned to restore peace, sanity and right relationship in our world otherwise we would not be here today. We need greatly to emphasise and to focus upon our common purpose. *This is the heart of the matter*. And we are pressured by time. There are those who set the world clock at 'four minutes to midnight' and have lately put it at 'three minutes to midnight'.

"Let us identify the essentials and drop the non-essentials. Let us listen inwardly and hear *what* each other is saying and not just *how* it is being said. Even within our own organisations there can, at times, be misunderstanding, conflict or dissension. This may be even more likely when various approaches to life meet together.

"What are the real issues here?

"Let us take one example of how the use of words can inflame or cause division. We have replaced all male-sounding words by such as 'chairperson' and so on. Certainly – most assuredly – women in our society have frequently been treated as 'second class citizens' and there is no doubt a need to provide equal opportunity, to address inequity. Often in society when injustices are being righted the balance can be overweighted to one side or the other by a vigorous pendulum swing. But if we all, men and women alike, learned to hear from within the heart of the matter, to stand at the centre, we would find no great objection, for instance, in the use of the word 'man' in its *generic* sense. We would find of greater importance the thought being conveyed rather than the focus on the words used. This is but one example and there are many *more* important ones. It is, however, a continuing bone of contention.

"There is no doubt that this adjustment in language needed to take place at the time since it is, of course, symbolic of a changing consciousness. Nevertheless, the fact of such necessity illustrates the powerful hold of the form world (including word forms and symbols in general) upon human consciousness. And let us always remember that any symbol ever places something between ourselves and reality. A symbol may hold interpretive value but nevertheless veils and hides the very reality we seek, that we would see face to face.

"Remember: As Christ advised, 'the Sabbath was made for man and not man for the Sabbath,' so language is made for humanity and not humanity for language.

"As individuals, groups and nations I am sure we all want peace and goodwill in our world. Why then does it seem such an incredibly difficult task to implement? Mainly because the world is afflicted by that great heresy – a belief in separateness. This in turn breeds distrust, fear, hatred, insecurity and misrepresentation of motive, to name just a few of our negative attitudes.

"But around the world today groups of people, like all of us here, are coming together with a *shared purpose*. There is a wide interaction – a networking of *group thought*. This can be a mighty force for constructive and creative change in attitudes and in action. A force that can even influence the decisions of governments."

Many meetings take place on inner planes at astral and mental levels in response to the needs of the work, as well as at those deeper levels of consciousness wherein we function with our inner group or Ashram. Not all workers maintain a conscious recollection of activity on the subjective planes. Undue focus upon the foreground of life is a common cause.

* * * * *

It is not possible in a book such as this to share any but isolated happenings and experiences from a journal of over 1600 foolscap pages. But throughout the time of the past thirty and more years the Group never slowed or ceased to move onward in deepening understanding and into the light and the service of the New Day in Aquarius.

The various phases of the group work are described in a general sense in the first book *Journey of a Lifetime*. Step by step together upon the Way the Group has arrived at a stage of its expression where former processes and methods of discovery are no longer necessary or relevant. Earlier processes give way to direct knowing. As described earlier in these pages the Group entered into the fifth phase of its living expression and learning proceeds within the Life aspect.

CHAPTER THIRTEEN
The Learning Process

For the circle has been well-nigh trod and the end approacheth the beginning.

We are told that in early days of the human race Members of Earth's Spiritual Hierarchy walked among the people and taught them the Mysteries of Life that held significance beyond the physical world and yet could be expressed through and within that world. The Hierarchy in turn had received these ancient Mysteries from the Great White Lodge on Sirius, the Brilliant Star of Sensitivity, of which Earth's Hierarchy is a lower reflection in the vast scheme of the Cosmos.

These ancient Mysteries contain the story of human destiny and bear great significance to us all at this moment in time. The world proceeds on its evolutionary path, cycle after cycle, and the human race moves onward as it is subjected to the varying energies and forces impinging upon consciousness and making impact upon the planet with all its kingdoms and systems governing growth.

At this moment in time we have arrived at the closing of one cycle and the opening of another as our planet moves out of the influence of Pisces and into the very different energies of Aquarius. There are many greater and lesser cycles in the scheme of things and we call the one mentioned an Age. It is during this time that the emergence of the Earth's Hierarchy is expected with its Members functioning openly once more upon the physical plane of living. The reappearance of their Great Leader, the Christ (by whatever name He is known in the world's religions), is awaited also with a lively expectancy. The ancient Mysteries will then be restored upon the planet.

There are many ways in which this restoration may take place, for the nature and type of Earth's peoples has such variation, as does the manner or mode of their expression. There will no doubt be, and already is, much teaching available to guide humanity the next step upon the upward way. However, in our time understanding must move on from the dependence on forms with the resultant outcome that we may observe in human affairs and expression across our world. We fail to realise that any form of teaching is only of use as it reveals to our conscious awareness the living process behind all forms, and consequently, just who we truly are and our role and purpose within the greater scheme.

The forms themselves must change progressively in order to accommodate advances and new possibilities emerging and coming within range as we proceed on our journey through time and place. This failure to understand the nature and purpose of form is the cause behind all separative attitudes and the resulting conflict so evident upon our planet.

In the coming time it will be understood that the Mysteries are not revealed alone by the teaching of information, albeit of universal principles, but may only be apprehended by the recognition of that which resides within ourselves. Our focus of consciousness must move from identification with the outer form life and move into the awareness of our energy body within which exist the energies with which we may work.

We must become directors of our own destiny as a vaster picture of our true birthright, our origins and our journey through time upon this planet reveals itself to our sight. At the same time we may become aware of our place in the greater scheme as we recognise the role of our planet within its exceedingly extensive and hitherto unrecognised relationships.

We can as yet only imagine what this realisation can mean in terms of human relationship within our world. We may discover that the tedious and never-ending process of working to restore balance, peace and sanity by addressing the effects – the visible results of separative attitudes and actions – will be rendered unnecessary as the many apprehend and embrace the understanding that humanity is one, the expression of spiritual being, and the varieties of type, culture, religion, etc. are but the living diversity of a human race in process of expression.

A member of the Group spoke of her experience in the business world:

"It is interesting how realisation appears to overwhelm us suddenly – such moments seem to occur in a single moment and yet must be the result of a process of gradually changing perception until, in that moment, the whole pattern towards which we have been moving suddenly is revealed – and then that pattern also is, at a later moment, seen as part of an even more all-embracing pattern of meaning and significance. The truth has been before us all along and yet the moment of 'seeing' is new.

"I was aware, during one of the last sessions of an outplacement training course for people whose jobs had just been made redundant, that a dynamic happens in a group in a classroom where integrating energy seems to flow through those who consciously work with the energies to draw the group together and also activate the potential in others. My realisation of this dynamic grew as I became aware of another person in the course who saw herself as a teacher of others and yet seemed to repel everyone. She was so self-centred that she saw everything and everyone through her own centre of the universe, distorted in a way that just did not meet or synchronise with anyone else's view. She ultimately moved to an isolated space while the others gathered within the energy flow.

"There was no personal will being applied but a will-to-good and a will-to-growth that was let loose to do its beneficent work. We allow it to flow through by our very recognition of it. It seems important to clearly identify the energies to allow the growth of the new expression. The new energies carry such a releasing freedom that allows for a new learning process to unfold for the individual and within the group."

Can we imagine our world if the next generation of children is taught according to the principles and the realities about which we have been speaking? May we visualise a new civilisation emerging built upon the foundations of a realised brotherhood of nations and of peoples? Are we able to anticipate the spiritual speed with which a new and more advanced and cooperative character will come forth into world expression, offsetting wastage of energy and misrepresentation of our true being in misguided, separative building? If so, our future is assured.

There are many of today's children who respond naturally to the new energies and the new teaching and there are those teachers who have the insight to guide them, draw out their potential and prepare them for their future roles and leadership. These teachers recognise that true education is gained through experience, the taking of responsibility and the ability to focus upon the essential and not upon external distractions. Knowledge is by no means neglected but it is understood as a part of the whole learning process in the development of balanced, rounded-out, responsible members of communities, moving through into wider spheres of expression.

A member of the Group spoke of her present experience teaching in a High School:

"Considering education and the youth of today, my view is that change is being forced on us by our children and their perceptions. Energetically they know they are free and they can't be forced to do anything they don't choose to. They are strong willed and have not yet experienced a need for respect or boundaries. We learned respect through fear. Our great challenge is: how do we give them an understanding of boundaries – respect, responsibilities and right relationships – in this new Aquarian age?

"As much as people may want to go back to the old ways,

more discipline, to have them do as they are told, we have to find new ways. I feel humanity is much further along the path with these wonderful energies coming in – and am always pondering my commitment 'to strengthen them within their soul' – some are so evolved with a strong soul link showing, others are developing the strong personality (a strong sense of self) needed for the soul to be interested, and others are just lost, reactive and experiencing life without control or rhyme or reason.

"As teachers the *trust* needed to be able to work energetically with students, fulfilling the soul's needs whatever that might be or mean, is the challenge. It requires a great trust of self, the ability to relate and to identify at that level and to open to the possibilities that are presented.

"It is the ability to go into the classroom with possible outcomes and ideas but the intention to work the energy and energies as best one can. Working group energy made up of many individual and needy students is the challenge. I was forced to rearrange one stream of the Year 7 Art classes halfway through the year. Very little learning was going on.

"We organised a Self Directed class, two Teacher Directed classes and one Opportunity-to-Learn class. It was so successful that all Year 7 classes are based on this format this year. We had the Primary Teachers identify students on this basis (prior to entering High School) so that next year we'll have two Self Directed classes and three Teacher Directed classes, one Literacy/Numeracy and one Opportunity-to-Learn class. The School has made a commitment to go ahead with this program. The Opportunity-to-Learn class has nine students and special programs have been written for these students – 'lost souls' who have difficulty relating to others or engaging in learning other than 'doing their own thing'.

"It was interesting this year because students knew where their energy fitted and they did not feel disadvantaged by the classes they were in. My great dislike of graded classes is that we are giving students expectations of their worth or worthlessness and I was worried that it may happen when I was forced to change the classes.

"I am continually questioning the principles and how they apply to education. The difficulty is to go out into 'the new' knowing that I don't know what it will look like because if I know, then it's the old – boy, is that trust and it's the best game in town!"

As we move through this transitional time and more fully into the new era, we may expect the newer intuitive ways to guide and express through the teaching and learning process. And indeed this planet of ours is a *schoolroom* in its every dimension, if we may but apprehend it and act upon that recognition.

A newsletter written by one member of the Group for the Christmas period 2001 defines clearly this transitional moment in time and the human challenge we all face to apprehend the issues and the opportunities. As we observe the past and the future revealed in the light of the present we are challenged to learn from this panoramic view of outmoded expression and of new and greater possibilities existing clearly before us, side by side. And then to move onward discarding all that needs to be left behind and that can retard the next movement in consciousness within the next cycle of our learning process.

This newsletter appears below.

Dear Friends,

As we enter the Christmas and New Year holiday season the annual pattern unfolds – commemoration of the past followed by celebration of the new. There is first a return to old connections; a re-uniting with old friends and family; a resurgence of tradition and historical connection and, for many, a reminder of our spiritual heritage. Timeworn rituals are observed in the present.

Then an expansive focus embraces all families, groups, nations and religions when they celebrate, as one, the promise of a new year. At this point we step beyond the reflective, backward-looking nostalgia and are freed into a new day and a fresh page on which to write the unfolding story of the divine nature manifesting in the world. On the one hand we are submerged in tradition and on the other we meet the future free of past care. We retain the essentials of our long history but a new vision replaces the burden of surface detail. The trauma of the past drops below our focus and a new future expands before us, redolent with promise and solution.

This magical moment has been portrayed dramatically in movies where the heroes, following some calamity such as shipwreck or road accident, suffer amnesia and forget who they have been up to this point – whether they are married, have children, were rich or poor, of honest or wicked bent. Yet they retain their sense of being in the world – they can speak and act appropriately and appear to retain all knowledge except that relating to their personal identity in the world. In many of these stories they are set free from past ill deeds and consequences. They are able then to live from a set of fresh and true values that seem to be automatically present despite the loss of many worldly layers that have been cultivated up to the moment of the trauma.

This new being they have become is unresponsive to any claims of the past and sees clearly and truly what is unfolding in the moment – wholly open to what life brings moment by moment and with a deeply inherent sense of truth. This new being is without prejudice, partisanship, preference, fears, doubts or debts. He stands at a point as though between incarnations, between worlds, where past experience is essentialised but does not veil insight into the next. This is a clue, perhaps, to that mysterious injunction: 'except you come as little children, you will not enter the kingdom of Heaven.'

The New Testament story of the rich young man not yet ready to move onward also points to the requirements of a new phase. We may understand this story in a deeper sense than the obvious meaning, on the outer surface of life, usually attributed to it. This young man's 'richness' was that of his wide-ranging sense of awareness, his aspiration and his developed faculties, resulting from his long, long evolutionary experience. The Christ tells him that he must leave behind his past achievements in order to be free to apprehend that which is beyond his present horizon and then to move forward the next step upon the way.

These injunctions point to a revelatory new moment of essential truth – a truth that cannot be changed or stripped away – the moment when spirit expresses in the world. The niceties of cultural, national, religious, social or familial convention and dogma are stripped away and things are seen for what they are in truth and in the eyes of God – terrible, awesome and wonderful. How *then* shall we be and act in the world?

At the traumatic impact of the attack on the World Trade Centre in New York (September 11th, 2001) the human world as a whole stood in that moment of shock, in amnesia, jolted out of the burden of past loyalties into a moment of clear sight unaligned with worldly expectations. Before the old familiar world began to flow back in to cloud vision once more everyone had been changed – many irrevocably. And it was said, 'The world will never be the same.'

So what is different? What touches us deeply that was previously unknown? What have we left behind? What new identity is revealed? The imagery and rhetoric with which we have described and circumscribed our view of the world is no longer able to define or contain our new experience of it – and yet language is our tool to anchor this shift in our experiential life. We are using old words but must re-define them even though they carry the danger of old understanding. Words such as business, war, economy, shares, military, religion, democracy, are being used in new contexts but can be dangerously misused allowing old prejudices and rationalisations to poison the metamorphosis. Yet there are new words ringing the changes with increasing resonance – unity, global, cooperation, interdependence, rights, human, mutual, freedom, responsibility.

In the moment between the past and a very different future, through this space between the worlds where only essential truth can be known, let us allow this liberating and empowering energy to do its beneficent work. We, in truth, have nothing to lose. We, in essence, are completely unencumbered. There is nothing real (or really nothing) that need drain away the living force, the enlivening energy that flows freely and equitably through all things, all people, all creation in the world.

It is a matter only of recognition, of realisation of the whole dynamic pattern and allowing a flow-through of the facilitating energy to draw out the best in all, for all. How simple! The new energies carry such a freedom for the individual potential *and* in harmony with the freedom of others' talents as well. The possessive acquisitiveness of the personal 'bottlenecks' or 'eddies' in the current are contained and bypassed by *seeing them clearly* and allowing the flow to bypass them and move on to its destined greatness. They will either realise or collapse under the pressure of the increased current – and ultimately come closer to their own realisation.

At this moment of the 'parting of the ways' we can be in danger of being sucked down by the undertow of the tide pulling back into old habits of living, thinking and feeling (and like the 'rich young man' turn sadly away) unless we, in our new objectivity, clearly distinguish them from the empowering energy of the new living water of Life that is pouring into a world thirsty for freedom. True discrimination is crucial.

The forces that would retard can be very close, even intimately so or integrally within otherwise 'worthy' activities with which we may be involved. We can be blinded by a mystical faith rather than knowing with a clear penetrating insight that will not balk at naming what it sees in order to empower what serves the whole or to refute a separative motive. A personal inclusiveness can be dangerous in the outer world of form where we can embrace a Judas and open the door on disruption and evil. Rationalisation may call white black and vice versa and so turn the key to evil. It can be a tool for good or evil and is no sure ground for confronting malign forces. The true difference lies at the point of motive and purpose behind the outer seeming and acts.

From the perspective of spirit we can differentiate between the old disciplines of good character values that a personality may pride itself on (be recognised for) and that new clarity of knowing what is true from the perspective of the whole. Glamour, untruth and evil have facility in the world of form and so, if we allow, can exploit our apparently 'good' qualities against us such as the blackmailer relying on a victim's love and loyalty, the ambitious man gaining position through good people's unwillingness to criticise, or the tyrant exploiting pacifism to speed his destructive course. For humanity harmony is *through* conflict and not by avoiding the necessary confrontation to identify, name and refute what is untrue. Harmony can only exist in *truth* and only in truth can there be freedom, empowerment and life.

Christ told us: 'I am the Way, the Truth and the Life. No man cometh unto the Father but by me.' We have also been addressed as 'Christ in you, the hope of glory.' This Christ aspect, this soul, this way to the immortal spirit, lives in the world through us. Such is the future fast approaching.

* * * * *

There is no way around it. Life on this Planet is, and has ever been, a learning experience and Life invites us, each and every one, to participate with a fully conscious awareness of the process, taking charge of our own destiny.

Let us stand then in conscious awareness at that 'midway point', between the past and the future, between spirit and matter, and lay hold of that essential truth of which the newsletter author speaks.

Let us understand what we have all learned, now distilled within us as our own true essence – that which has brought us to this present time – so freeing ourselves from the forms and structures which no longer have the capacity to make revelation in a new time. And let us embrace the understanding that those deeper Mysteries call to us from new horizons of awareness and of being.

Chapter Fourteen
Unfolding Realisation
The Fifth Phase of the Group

As we headed into the year 2002 the Group took stock of just where it stood. We considered the energies with and within which we were now operating. We observed our movement within the understanding of the Fifth Phase of the Group. We noted that the personality principles were well and truly superseded by those of the soul life and that the fifth phase could be seen to equate with the fifth kingdom of Soul. Working then within the Life aspect was a natural and inevitable movement onward.

Because we were operating within the Soul kingdom where Oneness exists and wherein energy flows freely between all beings, we began to understand more fully the principles that govern that state of Oneness and to observe an automatic flow between individuals and also between groups. If one group encountered certain difficulties or challenges in their work then the other group (or groups) who also understood these principles in operation found 'a call' from the group in need, and were aware of the required energies moving to assist and could cooperate in the conscious direction of these energies.

The group in need, or at least those within that group who were conscious of the process, were also able to access energies, at will, from the group reservoir. Clarification of issues and movement through into resolution of situations or advancement of the work was far more rapid and cut through unnecessary stages in a process. Of course, we do not need to point out that the foundations of these possibilities are focused in truth and trust.

We are beginning to recognise the annihilation of time as we observe the speed of response to the energies and the speed of the activity engendered as it works out in the outer world of expression. We are aware also that time cannot separate one group from another irrespective of location on the planet. Our working together is based in the subjective reality. It is understood that speed is assured as we move ahead and waste no time or effort in looking back at that which is left behind. Our energies are entirely focused in the work in hand.

Although at times certain of the group workers concerned meet together on the outer plane of life, the work performed is basically subjective in its nature. However, at this stage it seems useful to confer in outer contact on occasion. Apart from the particular form of service for which each group has taken responsibility, we are all aware of the important nature of the task that underlies and gives impulse to our unified operation and cooperation.

It is as we achieve such conscious awareness of one another and of the forces and energies involved in the work and those impinging upon the planet at this time, that a new possibility in human expression breaks through and can have an effect on human awareness as a whole. The new possibility is anchored in consciousness and upon the planet by the very fact of the group demonstration of its reality and of its actuality.

Just how may we define this 'possibility'? It is the realisation of the subjective realm that is our true habitat; it is identification with the Soul in all forms, in individuals and in groups. It recognises inter-soul relationship as we approach this work and understands the synthesis that underlies the forms.

We are dealing with the principles that govern the universe from the greatest to the small. As we work we are aware of these principles in operation. We are aware of the principle that governs all manifestation wherein we note a basic duality which, when unified, produces a third thus making a triplicity. We find this teaching, perhaps somewhat obscurely, in the teachings of the religions – such as that of the divine Trinity: Father, Mother and Son.

So we are finding a parallel in the working out of inter-group relationship as two groups have first entered into a close relationship and in terms of energy and awareness have merged in that they are completely aware of one another inwardly. There is no separation between them. The interplay of energies between each group serves to assist, complement and enliven the work of each and of the whole.

A third group, magnetically drawn and with obvious inner relationship with the other two, joins in the energy exchange. The energy of each group merges and synthesises and the three groups work together in unity. Very shortly members of these three groups will come together from around the world and meet together in the one place. It will be the first time that all three groups will be represented at the one time and in the one place. It is certain that further work and understanding will be established.

We can think of the extension of such activity as many groups grow in conscious understanding of the nature of subjective unity. No doubt there are many groups engaged in this movement within the world work however they may define the experience.

Those readers familiar with the meditative work of Triangles will recognise the same principle in operation. As co-workers make triangles of three people and link daily in thought and meditation they facilitate the inflow of the higher energies through the triangles and into human consciousness. The many triangles formed by these workers create a network of triangles in the etheric levels around the planet. The network is subject to continual extension as more co-operators join in this service activity. And so may it be with inter-group connections.

This principle may be seen expressing all the way from cosmic levels and has significance in the evolution of our planet, the solar system to which we belong and beyond. Is it any wonder that it is such a guide and that it breaks into our understanding as we function in group formation, and group with group, in the domain of our subjective reality?

In the deeper recesses of our knowing we are those workers who, consciously recognising the time has come, activate our original intention and come together on the outer plane to anchor the externalisation of new group activity. We all know as individual workers that we incarnated with a group purpose and so it is also of groups externalising at this moment to further the group work in Aquarius. So whether or not we may have recollection of subjective planning, the energies and forces of the moment are guiding these groups into right connection and outer contact to implement the next movement in the work.

As we enter this new time in Aquarius we are becoming aware of a movement in the teachings that will guide the human race upon the *next stage* of the Way. We are no longer so concerned about the fusion of the soul and the personality into one expressing unit, although that is a preliminary step. Now we see the goal as entrance into the Life aspect, the recognition that the earlier triplicity must resolve into that basic duality of spirit and matter. The Son or consciousness aspect gives way to the Father or the Monad, the Life aspect, and we recognise our relationship with the Father and our inevitable return to Him as we journey homeward.

* * * * *

Immediately following the completion of this chapter a member of one of the overseas groups which form an inter-group triangle of cooperation, reported the following experience:

"I linked up with my two triangle co-workers and visualised our triangle. We three merged and became one point of a triangle with our two inter-group triangle members from two other countries. Our three groups then merged into one point of a triangle with two other group clusters. I did not have a sense of the identity of the other two group points. They simply appeared as white spheres of light, as did our inter-group triangle.

"It appeared three dimensional, triangles within spheres, within triangles within spheres. The sense was that they kept forming larger triangles, which joined with other groups of triangles, not only around the planet but within the universe.

"This occurs to me as a universal principle revealing itself and it is hard to put into words. I drew a representation as best I could but cannot express the dimensionality of it. I didn't notice until I drew it that it resembled the Banner of Peace symbol, three balls within a sphere. In the meditation it continued to repeat within itself and I was within the structure."

* * * * *

Upon hearing the above, it was realised that at virtually the same time a Group member on this side of the planet experienced a similar meditation. Initially there was an awareness of the five planetary centres (London, Geneva, New York, Darjeeling, Tokyo) through which inlets it is known that energies enter our planetary life and consciousness. As usual, energies flowed from Darjeeling to our group centre Sydney. This flow was then seen to go *back and forth* between these two centres. A third point appeared and completed a triangle of energy. It was Tokyo. All seemed very active and activated. And news received later that morning from a co-worker in another country, telling of plans to visit and work with other groups in these centres, made it apparent that energies already established subjectively were proceeding to their anchorage in the outer world work.

Within a day or two there was a veritable explosion of contacts, group with group, across the planet, drawing us all closely and consciously together in a specific, united and free expression in service. On the inner plane, triangles of energy had been observed in process of forming, seemingly drawn by an irresistible magnetic force, manifesting through group relationships into the outer plane of expression. There was the impression that the world group was a participant in a forward movement of energies opening ahead of the human race.

At the same time there was the realisation that just as Hierarchy, so also the world group was required to work simultaneously upon the inner and the outer planes in recognition of the indivisibility of the planes that enliven and reveal humanity's life in all its dimensions of living expression. Our lives and our work ever manifest through the inner planes into outer expression and yet it is and has always been but one undivided unfoldment of the one life.

EPILOGUE

The Future World

The Day dawned bright and clear and the Sun followed its upward journey to its zenith. Full overhead the Sun shone down upon the Earth and upon its peoples and the shadows contracted close around the objects that cast them. No longer were the long, long fingers of the shadows claiming the world. No longer could those things that thrive in darkness find place.

All things were open to view. The world with all its kingdoms, with all its beings, was seen as One – a single living entity expressing the beauty and the wisdom of its diversity as the Logos had planned from the beginning.

All artificial divisions disappeared in the brilliance of the light. They were but the illusions caused when the forms stood in the way of the flood of light from the higher worlds. Forgetting they were the Children of the Father and believing they were the forms through which they lived and expressed, had been the major cause of human problems and misunderstanding throughout long Ages.

And yet it was the Father who originally had created the forms that, through their confinement and their power to endow experience, the Children might eventually awaken to their divine Sonship and thus fulfil their role as participants within the creative process of the life of the Logos of Planet Earth, their Father. Until such time, a youthful humanity had been protected from the fullness of light until it had learned the basic lessons in the school of planet Earth.

Now the turning cycles of the Cosmos brought this world into the influence of those energies through which the spiritual kingdom, the fifth Kingdom of the planet, could be apprehended and realised.

Ever since the time had come when the forces of truth and of error, of reality and of distortion, were of equal balance, the many grouped workers who stood together upon the spiritual path recognised that the Way lay open between the pairs of opposites, the opposing forces that drove the evolutionary Wheel of the planet.

They observed how those who still clung to their separated personal selves expressing selfishness, oblivious of the joy of Oneness, were as little wheels turning upon the planet and hindering the onward movement of the greater Wheel of humanity as it progressed through time and space.

The grouped workers had invoked the Light and the Enlightened Ones who dwelt therein to come to their aid as they endeavoured to bring Enlightenment to their world. They themselves worked without ceasing to express the realisation of the New Day.

As the Light increased within the world, as the Sun rose in the upper levels of human consciousness, the people were offered opportunity and challenge. That which was of the Light stood clearly evident but so also, by comparison, did that which was separated off from the advancing consciousness of the Race. Could humanity detach itself from this ancient and enormous thoughtform that contained the sum total of their experience and lesser identifications throughout time? They were challenged to rise, as the Phoenix, from the ashes of their previous selves, from the dead beliefs erased in the Light.

As the people struggled to adjust to the needed changes demanded by the incoming spiritual energies they began to realise that the answer was not to be found by devising outward changes. Unless there were basic changes *in consciousness* and the vaster horizon of Life was recognised, then the intended task would not be accomplished, and they could not enter the freedom of the fifth Kingdom to serve the plan of the new era together with their group.

In the meantime the *knowers* of the race continued to serve and stood as a bridge between the veil of forms in which their brothers still lingered, and the spiritual world. The Teacher who was to come looked upon his group of workers in the world and saw that their wills were merged with the greater Will and that they lived in goodwill for all. They were the *magnetic seed* of the future. They represented the assurance that the divine Plan of the Logos would not be thwarted by any lack of understanding of the people but now could move in unrestrained emergence to guide humanity on the next stage upon the Way.

The Sun poured forth its spiritual light and the grouped *knowers* of Aquarius, thinking ever in terms of response to the light of Life, and of service to the world, realised that the Teacher had never left them. He was known and seen by those who heard his sound. They worked beside him wielding the spiritual energies of the New Time as the Earth moved into the Age of Aquarius, the Server, to bring the soul in all into response and cooperation with the inner plan of the Logos.

And before long everyone will see Him.

* * * * *

This is by no means the end of the journey. There is ever a new beginning as together we move onward in conscious awareness.

* * * * *

All is well in the Kingdom, my friends